# BEAUTIFUL

# THINGS:

# OUT OF THE
# DUST

## Susan J Perry

# Copyright Page

Susan J Perry
Edgewater, Florida

*Simply This Publishing*

Kindle Direct Publishing

*"GOD said it,*
*I didn't,*
*GOD told me to tell you!"*

*~ Susan J. Perry ~*

*Ecclesiastes 3:11*
*He hath made every thing beautiful in*
*his time: also he hath set the world in*
*their heart, so that no man can find out*
*the work that God maketh from the*
*beginning to the end.*

## DEDICATION

Our dedication must always go to the Lord who is Alpha and Omega, First and the Last and my God. Bless the Lord O my soul Father, Son and Holy Ghost this book is yours front cover to back. All the contents of this book will be from you and for you from beginning to ending, you are the Author and Finisher of our faith, so that we may endure with you to the cross and know you have removed the shame and given us a place near the Throne with Jesus, our Savior. (Hebrews 12:2) Your books will be your inspiration.

God loves His people and He wants them encouraged, edified and happy to do the work of the Lord. Let's rededicate our lives and our story to Him today. He is so beautiful! He shall be glorified...

*Abba* this one is for you in all your beautiful ways...


## Thank You Lord!

# INTRODUCTION

God's creative beauty is within us; we are His creation. Although we look in the mirror daily and often shun the reflection there, we are His. When we criticize ourselves, especially among others we are criticizing God's creation. That's us.

God planted seeds of beauty within us from birth and now its harvest time. Let us learn to harvest the beauty from within. God starts with the heart; He searches our very motives and agendas. He is searching mine this very minute for the reason I am writing this book. It's just for you and if it helps just one or many than so be it but it is always for God's plan and purposes and not mine.

God often has me ministering to women. I will have ministered this word twice already as we will do it again in our church on Saturday, July 10th, 2010 this afternoon @ 2 PM titled: "Beautiful Things." We are going to attempt to draw the beauty out of women, because they have it on the inside and for some reason it is hidden deeply away because they have not drawn it out in so many, many years for fear someone might laugh at them. No, no what God has put on the inside of you is so beautiful that you will not recognize it when you actually see it.

God makes beautiful things. You have so much to share when you finally find it. Let's start taking a look now and we will find that hidden treasure buried deeply from the eyes of others. Love will draw you out...

Let us introduce you to God's beautiful things.

The evening of Saturday, July 10th, 2021 we found out our good friend and church sister, Margaret Showers went to the hospital with what the doctors have determined was a possible stroke. Our Pastors have rushed up to the hospital to pray and comfort the family. This woman is a notable woman of God and loved by all who know her. I made note of this today because I consider her one of those beautiful things God has created. She means so much to all of us. Now we will stand in prayer believing for her total healing by the hand of our mighty God. I am going to stand on this verse today:

*Psalm 107:20*
*He sent his word, and healed them, and*
*delivered them from their destructions.*

When Margaret recovers I will make note of the miracle here in this book for all to see. (Date & time); On Wednesday, July 14th, 2021 Margaret Showers came walking in our church doors to be with us in our Wednesday night service. Her faithfulness was undaunted as everyone sought God on behalf of her health and she received the miracle. Her husband Wayne was very glad to have her back and so were we, the church. Thank You Lord Jesus. This was one of those very beautiful things!! A miracle!

### *YAY GOD!*

  PS As of today, Wednesday, August 25th, 2021 Margaret has been out of the hospital for some time and has recovered nicely except some pain in her back from a spinal tap. If you think of it as you read this book, pray for her. She is home now and on the mend as we continue to pray for her.

# CHAPTERS INDEX

**Dedication**
**Page 5**

**Introduction**
**Page 6**

**Special Thanks...**
**Page 13**

**A Special Prayer**
**Page 14**

**A Special Friend**
**Page 16**

**Chapter 1: The Lord Makes Beautiful Things**
**Page 18**

**Chapter 2: How Beautiful is Your Heart**
**Page 23**

**Chapter 3: How Beautiful is The Blood**
**Page 28**

**Chapter 4: Beautiful Scriptures**
**Page 32**

**Chapter 5: Focus on Beautiful**
**Page 40**

**Chapter 6: Are You Dusty, Yet Beautiful**
**Page 45**

**Chapter 7: How Beautiful is Your Life**
**Page 50**

**Chapter 8: How Beautiful is The Fear of the Lord**
**Page 55**

**Chapter 9: Rise Up O' Woman of God/Man Of God**
**Page 61**

**Chapter 10: Forgiveness is Beautiful**
**Page 73**

**Chapter 11: What is More Beautiful Than Love**
**Page 78**

**Chapter 12: The Hallmark of Beautiful is Salvation**
**Page 82**

**Chapter 13: America the Beautiful**
**Page 90**

**Chapter 14: Peace Like a River**
**Page 94**

**Chapter 15: Honor is Beautiful**
**Page 100**

**Chapter 16: Repentance is Beautiful**
**Page 108**

**Chapter 17: Family is a Beautiful Thing**
**Page 113**

**Chapter 18: Trust In God is Beautiful**
**Page 121**

**Chapter 19: Mentorship is Beautiful**
**Page 127**

**Chapter 20: Prosperity is Beautiful**
**Page 131**

**Beautiful Things in a Dream**
**Page 141**

**A Beautiful Prayer**
**Page 144**

**Author's Corner**
**Page 146**

**Perry's Bookshelf**
**Page  149**

**Contact the Perrys**
**Page  152**

**Resources**
**Page  155**

# *Special Thanks...*

Thanks be to God and the women who make these books possible. We include all of mankind of course, thank you men too. We hope you will glean from this book as well. It is a grant from Heaven every time there is a new message I get to give out. Inspiration comes from the Holy Ghost within and so many who help us get this story told, thank you. You are so special. You are so beautiful. You are so loved.

An extra-special thanks to: **Felicia Utomi-Equere**, a wonderful friend of mine who mentored me many days, months, and years in prayer and devotion to God. It was in our time together when I realized God trusted me and I was growing in the things of the Lord. She guided me in a most sisterly way to stay on course when I was looking back and thinking about retreating. I had a long way to go and her mentorship was surely a foundation of just what I needed. She had Jesus; she had the Holy Ghost & Fire and she had a prayer language that would not quit and I want to honor her here. (And her husband Peter). She is what I call one of the most beautiful things in my life after Jesus. Thank you Felicia, my sister...

# A Special Prayer...

*Dear Father,*

*I come in the name of Jesus.*
*I bring your women to you today;*
*Those you have created and fashioned in your image Lord.*
*I ask you to renew a right spirit within them and refresh their souls today.*
*All those who are heavy laden Lord, lift off that spirit of heaviness and give them the garment of praise.*
*All those that need healing and deliverance, you sent your word to do the job and they will get exactly what they need.*
*Lord help them to remember they are beautiful inside and out;*
*And that they are your creation.*
*Father we need a special dose of the Holy Ghost today;*
*And we need your love in every way.*
*Cleanse us today of all unrighteousness and ungodly thoughts about ourselves.*
*Help us oh Lord to remember the cross of salvation that you saved us on that blessed day.*
*Father call us 'Beloved' again and take away all shame and guilt that has been lingering in our souls.*

*Father we forgive all those that have hurt us and we ask that you forgive us also for being so misguided.*

*Father we return to our first love and declare Jesus Christ is Lord over our lives and we will never turn away again for you are the only one true living God.*

*Oh thank You Lord for blessing each and every woman that turns the pages of this book.*

*Give them your favor as a shield as in Psalm 5:12 as they move forward in your strength Lord and their joy returns and their beauty spills out all over the place.*

*Show them that they are blessed to be a blessing.*

*They will glorify your name oh Jesus, Amen.*

## *A Special Friend...*

## Miss Queen Richardson

   My good friend, a very special life-friend was Miss Queen Richardson who passed from this world into eternal life on October 21, 2013 and I would like to remember her here. She was the epitome of a good friend and believer in Jesus Christ. When I arrived in Houston, Texas in 1980 I knew no one and as I started a job, Queen was the first to help me; see to me and mentor me. She was one of the first to tell me about Jesus although they were only seeds in the beginning, they grew eventually and we shared a lot later in our relationship together. She had a beautiful spirit.

After I moved on to Florida in 2003, we remained good friends by phone. I made sure she had some of my writings and we loved Jesus together. Her life overflowed on my life and she was one of the beautiful things that God put in my life that outshined any other. I will always love her. Sometimes I miss her terribly. She allowed me to share so many woes with her as I grew in the Lord and she always had an answer for me: *"Sue, wait on the Lord and be of good courage."* This was her answer for everything. This was hard for me. I should have heard her then, but I recognize her strength today and the love of God carried her each and every day. Thanks Miss Queen for all you sowed into me although sometimes it must've seemed fruitless. Now you got the victory with our Lord Jesus Christ! Still hoping our mansions are next to each others in heaven, praising God! Love you, so glad our lives touched one another's. It was beautiful memories.

# CHAPTER ONE

## The Lord Makes Beautiful Things

This book and story is based on Ecclesiastes 3:11, although the whole chapter is full of wisdom. Let's repeat the scripture here for definition:

*Ecclesiastes 3:11*
*He hath made every thing beautiful in his time: also he hath set the world in their heart, so that no man can find out the work that God maketh from the beginning to the end.*

We know God is our creator and we know He does fine work. So what is the problem? Let's break this scripture down by points and see where we are going in Ecclesiastes 3:11:

1.  He has made everything beautiful
2.  When? In his time (not ours)
3.  He set the world in our hearts
4.  So that no man could know all of the works of God
5.  Who will? God will from the beginning to the end.

Apparently the world in our hearts is God's plan, so we may not find out all about Him. Although we may want to know, I know that He has many mysteries and as Christians we keep digging to find out certain things that intrigue us. If you are not intrigued or at least interested in these mysteries, you may question your salvation or your love for God. When you love someone, normally you want to know more about them, day to day and year to year. This is how we go after God with zeal of finding those hidden treasures He has stored up for us.

Didn't Moses who was so close to God, say to Him, *"Lord show me your glory!"* As God hid him in the cleft of the rock, He allowed only His *'goodness'* to pass by Moses. And I know Moses must have been near to being bowled over by this sight and blinded by the great light that shone before His eyes. Think about that one. All glory unto God!

Moses was created to lead the Israeli people out of Egypt into the Promised Land. What are God's plans for your life and ministry? I know they are beautiful plans whatever they may be. You shall shine forth God's glory and remain beautiful in His eyes. He sees you; He loves you so much that He gave you Jesus to die for you and me.

I am reminded while writing this book that I had a mother a long time ago, she passed away in 1966 and I heard her voice as a young child saying:

1. "Beauty is only skin deep."
   And
2. "Suffer for beauty!"

These were harsh things to say over me as I think back upon it now. Those things were probably spoken over her as a young child and she never knew they were word curses. We just rebuke ALL word curses spoken over us right now by our family members and break the power of them totally in Jesus mighty name. See how the Holy Spirit brings things to our remembrance. He is so good. Let's address each one individually, I am sure you have some too if you think about it, think deeply now.

1. Beauty is only skin deep: no way because beauty is planted in our hearts. Beauty is on the inside of us as well as the outside and the depth of this beauty we do not know because the Creator put it there. So I rebuke that statement in Jesus name today! Remove it Lord!

2. Suffer for beauty: This is a horrible thing to say over anyone. I used to cry out loudly as

my mother would brush and comb my long blonde hair in the mornings before going out of the house each day. Speaking this thing over my head brought self-esteem issues at a young age but God is bringing it to my remembrance today which will then bring deliverance too because we have acknowledged it and now we rebuke that in Jesus name today! I say it ain't so; we remove that curse as far as it should go.

Please watch what you speak over others. These words will have a lasting effect good or bad. You are held accountable to God for all of your words.

Whatever you are remembering today that was spoken over you, write it down and then stand with Jesus and tear it up and give it all over to the Lord to heal and deliver you of all those word curses today! This is what the Bible says:

*Isaiah 54:17*
*No weapon that is formed against thee shall prosper; and every tongue that shall rise against thee in judgment thou shalt condemn. This is the heritage of the servants of the LORD, and their righteousness is of me, saith the LORD*

**Let's pray with you:**

*Dear Heavenly Father,*
*Bring word curses to this reader's memory and*
*remove them far from her and heal and deliver*
*her heart and soul from any harm that has*
*come unto her through these awful words. Lord*
*let us not curse anyone. Bless her with the oil of*
*gladness today as she goes forth healed in Jesus*
*name,*
*Amen.*

*Ecclesiastes 7:21-22*
*21 Also take no heed unto all words that are*
*spoken; lest thou hear thy servant curse thee:*

*22 For oftentimes also thine own heart knoweth*
*that thou thyself likewise hast cursed others.*

# CHAPTER TWO

## How Beautiful is Your Heart

Let's define beautiful in this second chapter:

**1:** having qualities of
beauty: exciting aesthetic pleasure

**2:** generally pleasing: EXCELLENT

I know some things about the heart and often times as a people, we do not know our own hearts. I am going to give you a few scriptures so that you will get the idea and meaning of what I am trying to convey here:

1. God searches the heart:

*Romans 8:27*
*And he that searcheth the hearts knoweth what is the mind of the Spirit, because he maketh intercession for the saints according to the will of God.*

2. Our hearts are wicked:

*Jeremiah 17:9*
*The heart is deceitful above all things, and*
*desperately wicked: who can know it?*

3. Our hearts are our lifeline:

*Proverbs 4:23*
*Keep thy heart with all diligence; for out of it*
*are the issues of life.*

4. Keep your heart from trouble:

*1. John 14:1*
*Let not your heart be troubled: ye believe in*
*God, believe also in me.*

AND

*2. John 14:27*
*Peace I leave with you, my peace I give unto*
*you: not as the world giveth, give I unto*
*you. Let not your heart be troubled,*
*neither let it be afraid.*

5. Repent and turn back to God:

*Psalm 51:10*
*Create in me a clean heart, O God; and renew a*
*right spirit within me.*

Please read Psalm 51 and ask God for help as David did and God will restore you if you think you have any heart issues at all. This Psalm is a cry unto God and He will hear you, I am sure. Our hearts need much searching and healing in this process of getting beautiful again. Our hearts carry things we have long forgotten and created trouble in that very vital organ. We need our hearts to live. That's why they are called 'vital organs.' We need a place our blood can flow through without hindrance or clogging as an obstacle in this life-flow. We must take care of our hearts as our very lives depend upon a good and healthy heart. Don't hold anything back, but allow God to expose every ugly thing that you may never have known about: old memories, old hurts; old disappointments and cares. Come on and give them all away. Be delivered and healed today, in Jesus mighty name.

If the Lord could do it for me, He will certainly do it for you, hold nothing back:

*Acts 10:34*
*Then Peter opened his mouth, and said, Of a truth I perceive that God is no respecter of persons:*

The Lord wants you to have a beautiful heart today as you gather your thoughts and cares to give them to Him, gladly. We willingly serve God and love Him and He wants to care for your beautiful heart and extend your life in Him, cleansed and set free as when you were born. Yes we were born into original sin, but our hearts were not troubled yet until those cares came upon us. Until that abuse hurt you; until your misguided parents spoke wrong words over you and you hid it in your little heart, far, far away. These kind of deep wounds from childhood manifest long-time hurt. Now maybe you were raised up with the best of everything and never were hurt as a young child which seems highly unlikely because even my husband John who lived an idyllic life in his childhood was hurt by the kids who rejected him or mocked him in some way. We all get something thrown at us from time to time. These are the tests and trials of life. What does the Word say about this? We will get a crown in Heaven:

*James 1:12*
*Blessed is the man that endureth temptation:*
*for when he is tried, he shall receive the crown*
*of life, which the Lord hath promised to them*
*that love him.*

How sweet and beautiful is this? Upon arriving to Heaven we shall receive a crown of life and we

are blessed to endure these temptations today.
God's promises are for those of us who love Him.
I know you must love Him or you would not be
reading this book. God is changing your heart
today.

## Let's pray with you:

*Dear Heavenly Father,*
*We come in the name of Jesus:*
*To pray for hearts today;*
*Lord, heal the broken-hearted and mend their*
*souls accordingly.*
*We rejoice for your healing and deliverance*
*today as we pray.*
*Please create in these women, new hearts of*
*flesh instead of stone.*
*Thank You Lord for all you do to get us*
*beautiful and in position for your blessing.*
*We love you,*
*Amen.*

# CHAPTER THREE

## How Beautiful is The Blood

Oh the blood, the blood of Jesus, how beautiful is the blood shed on Calvary for us.

*1 John 1:7*
*But if we walk in the light, as he is in the light, we have fellowship one with another, and the blood of Jesus Christ his Son cleanseth us from all sin*

There are songs sung about the Blood of Jesus; there are proverbs written and poetry and books too. Prayers are said applying the Blood of Jesus; nothing can escape the blood. It is life giving; it is sin erasing. Our lives and our salvation depend upon it; we got it at that old rugged cross as they hung Jesus to die for us. His blood was shed for us and blood is precious. We cannot exist without blood or its qualities. We need it. Here is how we know:

*1. John 6:53*
*Then Jesus said unto them, Verily, verily, I say unto you, Except ye eat the flesh of the*

Son of man, and drink his blood, ye have no life
in you.

2. Ephesians 2:13
But now in Christ Jesus ye who sometimes were
far off are made nigh by the blood of Christ.

3. Hebrews 10:19
Having therefore, brethren, boldness to enter
into the holiest by the blood of Jesus,

4. Hebrews 12:24
And to Jesus the mediator of the new covenant,
and to the blood of sprinkling, that speaketh
better things than that of Abel.

5. Hebrews 13:20
Now the God of peace, that brought again from
the dead our Lord Jesus, that great
shepherd of the sheep, through the blood of the
everlasting covenant,

6. 1 Peter 1:2
Elect according to the foreknowledge of God the
Father, through sanctification of the Spirit, unto
obedience and
sprinkling of the blood of Jesus Christ: Grace
unto you, and peace, be multiplied.

*7. 1 John 1:7*
*But if we walk in the light, as he is in the light,*
*we have fellowship one with another, and*
*the blood of Jesus Christ his Son cleanseth us*
*from all sin.*


*8. Revelation 1:5*
*And from Jesus Christ, who is the faithful*
*witness, and the first begotten of the dead, and*
*the prince of the kings of the earth. Unto him*
*that loved us, and washed us from our sins in*
*his own blood,*

Scripture from the Word of God reveals the truth about the blood. This is our covenant with our Father in Heaven, and Jesus is the New Covenant which is so much better than the old. We no longer have to sacrifice animals and shed their blood to atone for our sins but we have Jesus who died and fully atoned for all our sins through His blood and sacrifice on the cross. He gave life; He died and in three days was resurrected to be seated at the right hand of the Father today. We too are made beautiful by the shedding of the blood of Jesus Christ cleansing us and making us white as snow:

*Isaiah 1:18*
*Come now, and let us reason together, saith*
*the LORD: though your sins be as scarlet, they*

*shall be as white as snow; though they be red*
*like crimson, they shall be as wool.*

How beautiful is the blood Jesus making us beautiful today for all He did on the cross belongs to us. We say and believe that we have the DNA of Jesus and His blood flows through our veins. If they took a blood test today and checked for heredity they would find Jesus in the blood; at least in my blood. How about yours? Now let us go forward knowing we are beautiful...


**Let's pray with you:**

*Dear Heavenly Father,*
*We pray in the name of Jesus:*
*We apply the blood of Jesus to all;*
*And we thank you for all Jesus did on the cross.*
*We have so much to be thankful for now,*
*The blood, the blood and the blood,*
*Shall redeem our families and protect all*
*of us too.*
*We praise and worship you;*
*Amen.*

# CHAPTER FOUR

## Beautiful Scriptures

*Psalm 48:2*
*Beautiful for situation, the joy of the whole*
*earth, is mount Zion, on the sides of the north,*
*the city of the great King*

*Song of Solomon 6:4*
*Thou art beautiful, O my love, as Tirzah, comely*
*as Jerusalem, terrible as an army with banners.*

*Song of Solomon 7:1*
*How beautiful are thy feet with shoes, O*
*prince's daughter! the joints of thy thighs are*
*like jewels, the work of the hands of a cunning*
*workman.*

*Isaiah 4:2*
*In that day shall the branch of*
*the LORD be beautiful and glorious, and the fruit*
*of the earth shall be excellent and comely for*
*them that are escaped of Israel.*

*Isaiah 52:1*
*Awake, awake; put on thy strength, O Zion; put on thy beautiful garments, O Jerusalem, the holy city: for henceforth there shall no more come into thee the uncircumcised and the unclean.*

*Isaiah 52:7*
*How beautiful upon the mountains are the feet of him that bringeth good tidings, that publisheth peace; that bringeth good tidings of good, that publisheth salvation; that saith unto Zion, Thy God reigneth!*

*Jeremiah 13:20*
*Lift up your eyes, and behold them that come from the north: where is the flock that was given thee, thy beautiful flock?*

*Jeremiah 48:17*
*All ye that are about him, bemoan him; and all ye that know his name, say, How is the strong staff broken, and the beautiful rod!*

*Ezekiel 16:12*
*And I put a jewel on thy forehead, and earrings in thine ears, and a beautiful crown upon thine head.*

*Ezekiel 16:13*
*Thus wast thou decked with gold and silver;*
*and thy raiment was of fine linen, and silk, and*
*broidered work; thou didst eat fine flour, and*
*honey, and oil: and thou wast*
*exceeding beautiful, and thou didst prosper into*
*a kingdom.*

*Ezekiel 23:42*
*And a voice of a multitude being at ease was*
*with her: and with the men of the common sort*
*were brought Sabeans from the wilderness,*
*which put bracelets upon their hands,*
*and beautiful crowns upon their heads.*

*Acts 3:2*
*And a certain man lame from his mother's*
*womb was carried, whom they laid daily at the*
*gate of the temple which is called Beautiful, to*
*ask alms of them that entered into the temple;*

*Acts 3:10*
*And they knew that it was he which sat for alms*
*at the Beautiful gate of the temple: and they*
*were filled with wonder and amazement at that*
*which had happened unto him.*

*Romans 10:15*
*And how shall they preach, except they be sent?*
*as it is written, How beautiful are the feet of*

*them that preach the gospel of peace, and bring
glad tidings of good things!*

These are not just random scriptures but are
the very description given from the Throne
Room of Heaven that our lives; yes your lives are
beautiful in Jesus Christ who lived and died for
us. Now we live in Him gaining so much more
beauty without measure as our life radiates for
Him and from Him and through Him. Our lives
are rich and beautiful because of Jesus Christ;
only because of Him.

As a Christian I have always thought about the
Gate Beautiful that the lame man met Peter and
John at begging for alms each and every day.

*Acts 3:1-9*

*1 Now Peter and John went up together into the
temple at the hour of prayer, being the ninth
hour.*

*2 And a certain man lame from his mother's
womb was carried, whom they laid daily at the
gate of the temple which is called Beautiful, to
ask alms of them that entered into the temple;*

*3 Who seeing Peter and John about to go into
the temple asked an alms.*

*4 And Peter, fastening his eyes upon him with John, said, Look on us.*

*5 And he gave heed unto them, expecting to receive something of them.*

*6 Then Peter said, Silver and gold have I none; but such as I have give I thee: In the name of Jesus Christ of Nazareth rise up and walk.*

*7 And he took him by the right hand, and lifted him up: and immediately his feet and ankle bones received strength.*

*8 And he leaping up stood, and walked, and entered with them into the temple, walking, and leaping, and praising God.*

*9 And all the people saw him walking and praising God:*

I have thought as long as I have studied that this was a picture of salvation in the Bible. The lame man represents us while we were yet sinners and Jesus came to save us. The lame man was begging for alms; for provision each and every day someone would carry him to this gate. Imagine that: each and every day this man lame from birth or his mother's womb, the scripture says was carried and sat at the gate Beautiful. Every day he was introduced to salvation but instead he begged for alms totally missing each opportunity. Instead, the people going in and out gave him mere alms to satisfy him in his lame condition. What condition are we in when we do not know Jesus? We are like the lame man, we cannot walk right until we walk with Jesus in salvation, and do we walk uprightly as He does or as God has intended for us? We should check our walk today.

What Peter and John offered this man was not only healing in the ability to physically walk but also to walk upright spiritually in the salvation that was offered. You know this man got saved as well as healed, don't you?

Look at this lame man in one other aspect of his character as he sat and begged; my husband pointed this out to me as I hurriedly gave him my revelation about these scriptures. It says in verse 5 after Peter and John told him to *"Look on us,"* in verse 4,

5. *And he gave heed unto them, expecting to receive something of them.*

This lame man EXPECTED to receive something from these men. His heart was open and ready to receive whatever they had to offer him. And as he expected he did not get alms but he got healing, deliverance; he got it all in his salvation package offered to him at this gate Beautiful. He got more than he was expecting; how much money can buy all that he received that day? *"Silver and gold have I none,"* says Peter to the lame man in verse 6. And Peter gave this man all that he had promised and all that he had to give. Then this man walked into the temple leaping and praising God for all he received at the gate. Wow what a tale of salvation! Isn't that how we feel when we have our first *'Come to Jesus meeting'*? We come to the gate Beautiful as God makes everything beautiful in its time. (Ecclesiastes 3:11)

Then there is the dung gate of sin which we come from before we enter into the gate Beautiful of salvation. It has many ugly qualities until we meet the King of kings and the Lord of lords and He makes everything beautiful in his time.

*Nehemiah 2:13*
*And I went out by night by the gate of the valley, even before the dragon well, and to the dung port, and viewed the walls of Jerusalem, which were broken down, and the gates thereof were consumed with fire.*

Nehemiah a re-builder of the Wall of Jerusalem which was destroyed by fire had to be recon-structed. If we read this scripture in Nehemiah

2:13, this is a picture of our lives without Jesus in salvation. We are broken down and the dragon (satan) is at the well of our lives. We are in a pile of dung because nothing is good without Jesus. So they come to rebuild those walls of salvation that had been broken down over the years. Now we are headed to the gate Beautiful, hand in hand with Jesus as He rebuilds our lives in a most beautiful way.

GOD MAKES EVERYTHING BEAUTIFUL IN HIS TIME!

## Let's pray with you:

*Dear Heavenly Father,*
*Thank you for our salvation in Jesus;*
*We are so grateful for all you do for us.*
*We are beautiful because of Jesus,*
*And the blood He shed on Calvary.*
*Thank You Lord!*
*Thank You for your timing in my life;*
*We are at the gate Beautiful.*
*You have blessed me,*
*Cleansed me and made me whole.*
*In Jesus precious name,*
*Amen.*

# CHAPTER FIVE

## Focus on Beautiful

The Bible says women are beautiful like gems or good things. Let us mimic the Bible and have a heart after God's heart and our perspective will change, certainly. Let us keep our eyes upon Jesus who makes us beautiful every day. We see through His all-seeing eyes and loving heart.

In Genesis 29:17 it says: *Leah was tender eyed; but Rachel was beautiful and well favoured*

These were Jacob's wives and comparatively very different.

In Deuteronomy 21:11 it says:
*And seest among the captives a beautiful woman, and hast a desire unto her, that thou wouldest have her to thy wife;*

Here it is talking about the captives among Israel, the women must have been beautiful and the men could take them as wives if they desired.

In 1 Samuel 16:12 it says: *And he sent, and brought him in. Now he was ruddy, and withal of a beautiful countenance, and goodly to look to. And the LORD said, Arise, anoint him: for this is he.*

Here the Bible is speaking of David, the young shepherd boy they later anointed King. I can tell that by the text here.

In 1 Samuel 25:3 it says: *Now the name of the man was Nabal; and the name of his wife Abigail: and she was a woman of good understanding, and of a beautiful countenance: but the man was churlish and evil in his doings; and he was of the house of Caleb.*

This scripture in the Bible speaks of Abigail taken by David later to wife after her nasty husband, Nabal died.

In 2 Samuel 11:2 it says: *And it came to pass in an eveningtide, that David arose from off his bed, and walked upon the roof of the king's house: and from the roof he saw a woman washing herself; and the woman was very beautiful to look upon.*

King David loved a beautiful woman and here he was tempted by Bathsheba bathing on her rooftop, unclad. He later repented of his sin but married the woman after killing her prominent husband so he could have this beautiful woman for himself.

In Esther 2:7 it says: *And he brought up Hadassah, that is, Esther, his uncle's daughter: for she had neither father nor mother, and the maid was fair and beautiful; whom Mordecai, when her father and mother were dead, took for his own daughter.*

Esther was seen as a beautiful woman who came to prepare to marry King Xerxes who had deposed his wife Queen Vashti due to her disobedience. She was a chosen woman among many, many brought to tempt the King and he chose Esther or Hadassah which was her Hebraic name.

Here in these beautiful scriptures we are focusing on the natural beauty of a woman and not the inner beauty which goes a little deeper.

God created woman for man to love and cherish and to procreate also. There is a scripture in Proverbs that I find intriguing as we talk about beauty:

*Proverbs 18:22*
*Whoso findeth a wife findeth a good thing, and obtaineth favour of the LORD.*

Here apparently is what is valuable to God as it says this in scripture:

*Proverbs 31:30*
*Favour is deceitful, and beauty is vain: but a woman that feareth the LORD, she shall be praised.*

AND

*1 Peter 3:3-4*

*3 Whose adorning let it not be that outward adorning of plaiting the hair, and of wearing of gold, or of putting on of apparel;*

*4 But let it be the hidden man of the heart, in that which is not corruptible, even the ornament of a meek and quiet spirit, which is in the sight of God of great price.*

Focusing on beauty may be in vain as you look upon one's countenance but looking on one's heart as God does may produce a different story. There is so much I have written about women and for women and although I am no expert by any means, I think I know them a little bit. We are still researching. We are still gleaning from many fields as Ruth did in the Bible. We must know a subject before we can teach it or write about it and 'Beautiful Things' is a favorite topic of mine. It makes so many happy and smile.

**Let's pray with you:**

*Dear Heavenly Father,*
*Thank You for all these beautiful women;*
*Thank You for their countenance;*
*Thank You for their hearts.*
*You have created great things,*
*And we are grateful for each and every one.*
*We pray in Jesus beautiful name,*
*Amen.*

# CHAPTER SIX

## Are You Dusty, Yet Beautiful

*Genesis 2:7*
*And the LORD God formed man of the dust of the*
*ground, and breathed into his nostrils the*
*breath of life; and man became a living soul.*

Imagine that Father God formed us from the
dust of the earth. We are made of terra firma.
Now that is man and wo-man is formed from
that rib of Adam's side, never to be parted or left
again in the dust. When Adam and Eve sinned in
the Garden of Eden, God cursed them as He gave
them their punishment which wasn't pretty. But
God was merciful. Here is what He said to that
old serpent that did all the tempting:

*Genesis 3:14*
*And the LORD God said unto the serpent,*
*Because thou hast done this, thou art cursed*
*above all cattle, and above every beast of the*
*field; upon thy belly shalt thou go,*
*and dust shalt thou eat all the days of thy life:*

He sent him back to the dust and made him to crawl on his belly all of his days. He was made a lowlife, as low as the dust for his scheme in things. And then another curse came a few scriptures later saying:

*Genesis 3:19*
*In the sweat of thy face shalt thou eat bread, till thou return unto the ground; for out of it wast thou taken: for dust thou art, and*
*unto dust shalt thou return.*

Adam and Eve were cursed to the dust that when they died they would return to the dust and be buried. That's why so many say dust to dust, and it was all about Adam and Eve pertaining to that original sin they got caught up into. And God continued to curse them down in their generations too:

*Genesis 13:16*
*And I will make thy seed as the dust of the earth: so that if a man can number the dust of the earth, then shall thy seed also be numbered.*

Dust happens throughout the Bible. How dusty can we be as we look up and focus on Heaven? Brush the dust off because God has made you a brand new creation as you came to Jesus in salvation. Isn't that fact truly beautiful? God makes beautiful things out of the dust. He created man in this way.

Jesus talks about dust pertaining to rejection as we go out and preach the good news of the gospel:

*Matthew 10:14*
*And whosoever shall not receive you, nor hear your words, when ye depart out of that house or city, shake off the dust of your feet.*

Apparently their walk on the earth was very dusty. They didn't have nice paved roads as we do today, nothing but dirt and rock. They walked in the dust.

During times of great duress, men and women of God would rend their garments and put on sackcloth and ashes (or dust). Mordecai did this when he heard the news that Haman put out a proclamation or law to execute the Jews due to Mordecai's own disobedience before him. He would not bow down to anyone but our God. This caused much commotion in this Kingdom of Persia during Esther's time. She was aware that they were about to annihilate her entire race of people. Esther who was married to the King and found favour with him fasted and prayed and the God she served helped her. But Mordecai being her uncle feared retribution for his disobedience to this new law of bowing countered with giving Queen Esther the ball to run with and they eventually did win the game. The Jews lived and Haman and his family died. Here it is in Esther 4:1:

*When Mordecai perceived all that was done, Mordecai rent his clothes, and put on sackcloth with ashes, and went out into the midst of the city, and cried with a loud and a bitter cry;*

This was a sign of grief or great stress about the tyranny of those times. We should all be in Washington, DC right now sitting at the City Gate rending our garments in sackcloth and ashes for what is going on in our country. Evil is trying to take over but God has chosen this country of America to be free and serve Him fully. We must continue to obey.

America the beautiful, land where I live; The United State of America is so beautiful and the ugly is trying to overrun this great nation. God will see to us and cause enmity between them and us forever.

Everyone who has ever lived here or visited here agrees this land is beautiful from sea to shining sea. That's why we have so many immigrants trying to get here and become citizens. It's been going on for many, many years from all different countries. There is no other place I would rather live. America is one of those beautiful creations of God that we are privileged to stand on and partake of its blessing.

One day we will all go back to the dust for whence we came and go to be with Father in Heaven who makes all things beautiful in His time. (Ecclesiastes 3:11) He sure knows how to keep us. He keeps us beautiful! If you are concerned about the dust factor then you have a long way to go, come to Jesus and know that He is the way, the truth and the life and by no other means may we come to the Father but by Him. It may be a dusty road you are traveling right now but by the time you get there, you will know that everything is beautiful in its time made by God.

**Let's pray with you:**

*Dear Heavenly Father,*
*We come in the beautiful name of Jesus,*
*We pray for all who are here today,*
*And may need a helping hand up;*
*To find the right path of life for herself;*
*Help her Lord and guide her from the dust,*
*To Your marvelous light.*
*Thank You Lord for doing that,*
*Amen.*

# CHAPTER SEVEN

## How Beautiful is Your Life

There is so much to be thankful for today as we move forward, never looking back. God has made our lives beautiful in His time and we continue to grow and love all that He surrounds us with.

Just listening to worship declaring the name of Jesus is beautiful; we have perfumes named this and we can just look around and find something that is beautiful for sure. God created it all.

Life is beautiful... Think about the birth of a child; a new job; a new book to read; a new adventure; a new friend; a new church to join and all the beautiful things God gives us in this path called life. All things endure when coming from God, because He makes all things beautiful in His time.

The seasons are beautiful, each known for the timing of God and all different. Each day given us is new and exciting. Like the colors of the rainbow, they each have different hues and shadings to give you many, many facets in your journey. God is a giver of good things! Breath for instance: each one is important and needed to live, so God supplies each one.

*Job 33:4*
*The spirit of God hath made me, and*
*the breath of the Almighty hath given me life.*

Even Job found out this thing about breath. See this in this scripture above. Job knew he needed his breath for life and where it had come from, it came from the Almighty. Each day is beautiful as we take breaths without even thinking about it at all. It's natural, it's part of life. Isn't it, we just take it for granted until we get sick or diseased and we no longer have as much breath to breathe each day. Our bodies get sick because our oxygen levels are lower than usual. If you have ever noticed the doctors and the nurses check a patients 'oxygen levels.' I thank God for mine so far.

Before I met Jesus I was an addicted smoker and it took a miracle of God to refuse another cigarette. I had a big problem but when God saved me, He started to deliver me, and today I have little trouble with my breathing. I am so thankful for that. My lungs have been x-rayed several times to find them clear but with some scar tissue to remind me never to go back to that old way of life. We need our breath, stay thankful. When a body dies in that final moment the breath is taken away, and the rest of that process follows. The spirit of a man leaves the body and it leaves via the mouth; in the breath as it goes. God first breathed life into us as His Spirit and received it back to Himself in our earthly deaths as we resurrect unto Him; forevermore.

How beautiful is breath? Have you ever seen it on a cold window before? We used to do that on cold days in Upstate New York when we were kids, just playing around. But we didn't know anything about breath or its importance but we just kept doing it. Now as elders we realize the importance of each and every breath we take and we guard our lives as significant and created by our God. It took a long time for me to ever realize that. What did God promise us in Psalm 91, a great Psalm to read and study?

*Psalm 91:16*
*With long life will I satisfy him, and shew him my salvation.*

Yes this is one of God's promises, I found one in Psalm 91 which is filled with God's goodness, check it out for yourself.

The promise is long life; God will satisfy us as He guides us into salvation. This is a beautiful tour I am on right now with the Lord. His Word is sure and I am quite satisfied with my life today. He has me writing so you can read and glean in our field of glory. *Long life...*

How long will be satisfactory to you? Maybe 50~60~70~80~90~100, well you choose with the Lord. This is a question many have asked but we should not know that day or the hour that the death of our bodies will come knocking on our doors but kept in beautiful suspense until that day comes. Then we will know I am sure. I am heading for number 70 and God has blessed and favoured me in so many ways. We often hear the familiar statement of: *"God works in mysterious ways."* Although it is just a saying of man, we know this by experience. We just went over that in prior chapters in Ecclesiastes 3:11. God does not want us to know ALL of His ways, no not yet at least but one day we will go to be with Him for all eternity and then we will know that we know....

**Our lives will be totally beautiful!**

## Let's pray with you:

*Dear Heavenly Father,*
*I pray in the name of Jesus;*
*I pray all who read this live this life beautiful.*
*Thank you for every one who needs You.*
*Thank You Lord for Beautiful Seed today;*
*We love You,*
*Amen.*

# CHAPTER EIGHT

## How Beautiful is the Fear of The Lord

This was spoken to me while driving my vehicle yesterday by the Lord, *"Fear of the Lord is beautiful."* It was with a sincere and lovely voice that God spoke to me. There is so much about God that is beautiful, but fear of the Lord is special. I have known this for many years but it really struck a compassion cord with me when the Lord said this to me, this way. I guess it hit the cord He wanted to hit, right on target. There are just some things you do expect to call beautiful but God's ways are not our ways exactly. Let's define it first:

## Fear of the Lord:

It is in the Old Testament used as a designation of true piety (Proverbs 1:7; Job 28:28; Psalms 19:9). It is a fear together with love and hope, and is therefore not a slavish dread, but rather filial reverence. (Compare Deuteronomy 32:6; Hosea 11:1; Isaiah 1:2; 63:16; 64:8.) God is called "the Fear of Isaac" (Genesis 31:42; Genesis 31:53), i.e., the God whom Isaac feared.

A holy fear is enjoined also in the New Testament as a preventive of carelessness in religion, and as an incentive to repentance. (Matthew 10:28; 2 Corinthians 5:11; 7:1; Philippians 2:12; Ephesians 5:21; Hebrews 12:28-29). (From Bible.Dictionary.com)

*2 Corinthians 5:11*
*Knowing therefore the terror of the Lord, we persuade men; but we are made manifest unto God; and I trust also are made manifest in your consciences.*

The fear of the Lord is a reverence or honor for Him that exists no where else but only for our Holy God. The Lord thinks this is beautiful. I tend to agree with Him today because He must want me to write about it if it were not so. Let's dive into some of the scriptures that I love especially in the five wisdom books of Job, Psalms, Proverbs, Ecclesiastes and Song of Solomon. Everything is beautiful in Christ Jesus our Lord.

*Job 28:28*
*And unto man he said,*
*Behold, the fear of the LORD, that is wisdom;*
*and to depart from evil is understanding.*

*Psalm 25:14*
*The secret of the L*ORD *is with them*
*that fear him; and he will shew them his*
*covenant.*

*Proverbs 1:7*
*The fear of the L*ORD *is the beginning of*
*knowledge: but fools despise wisdom and*
*instruction.*

*Proverbs 9:10*
*The fear of the L*ORD *is the beginning of*
*wisdom:*
*and the knowledge of the holy*
*is understanding.*

*Proverbs 10:27*
*The fear of the L*ORD *prolongeth days:*
*but the years of the wicked shall be shortened.*

*Proverbs 14:27*
*The fear of the L*ORD *is a fountain of life, to*
*depart from the snares of death.*

*Proverbs 15:33*
*The fear of the L*ORD *is the instruction of wisdo*
*m; and before honour is humility.*

*Proverbs 16:6*
*By mercy and truth iniquity is purged: and*
*by the fear of the L*ORD *men depart from evil.*

Many good things are happening to those who fear the Lord and hold Him high in great reverence. He is the Most High God. We can do nothing without Him. (John 15:5) I remember many times remarking to folks that I have too much fear of the Lord to go back to my old way of life. My life is so beautiful now. Can we have too much fear in the Lord, somehow I doubt it. But it sounds good. You can never have too much of God. He is our everything.

According to these above scriptures the fear of the Lord is many times the beginning of something good like knowledge and wisdom as in Proverbs 1:7 and Proverbs 9:10. I believe this fear of Lord comes upon you in salvation and we need it to perfect our walk with Father. It keeps our love and respect in check before His Throne of Grace. Our hearts must be right before Him as we pursue the Christ-like life we are on a journey with. Sin suddenly falls off of us; our old man passes away and we become more like the image of God He created us to be. It is not a physical likeness because we all look so different but it is the spiritual likeness that we become more like Him and that is certainly beautiful.

Through the fear of the Lord our understanding changes and our wisdom increases as we read and study the Word; as we pray and fellowship with God daily. Our life in Him grows and matures. The fear of the Lord helps us to come under His authority and stay there. God is sovereign and the more we realize that, the more we will be blessed. The Bible says we have two choices: Be blessed or be cursed. Ask Adam and Eve who sinned and were thrown out of the garden. Which is better? Let us walk in the blessing of the Father ~ that is beautiful!

   Do you remember as a young child how wonderful your parents were to you especially if you were behaving and staying within the boundaries of their house rules? Love was very evident. When you disobeyed you felt terrible with a lot of guilt and shame. So thankful we have a forgiving Father in Heaven today. Jesus our Savior has given us the option of forgiveness and is our beautiful thing. Oh Jesus is beautiful every single moment of every single day...

## Let's pray with you:

*Dear Heavenly Father,*
*We thank you for Jesus,*
*We come in His mighty name to pray.*
*Lord help us to have the fear of the Lord more*
*and more;*
*As we seek you; as we love you,*
*Please help us.*
*You said it is beautiful;*
*Make us beautiful today Father,*
*You created us in your image.*
*We surrender all to you.*
*Amen.*

# CHAPTER NINE

## Rise Up O' Woman of God

I have been using this particular statement about women for years. The author is unknown and I have gone again today online to research it and there is nothing like this out there. There are few poems but this is more like a statement from God. It is an amazing work encouraging women and I love to use it and I pray it is not someone else's copyright, I have checked and checked. So here it goes remembering you are one of God's beautiful things made from the dust:

## Rise Up O' Woman of God...

You are passing over the Jordan into the Promised Land, I have prepared for you and I have guided you. Each word that I have given you was a preparation, like the manna that I gave to the children of Israel. And like the children of Israel you have become very weary at times, of the manna. But this was to feed you and sustain you.

Now, I AM taking you from your wilderness and into your Promised Land. I will go with you...I will go before you...And I will go behind you and be your rear guard. You shall move into the land that I have prepared you as you draw near to the river to go into the place that I have called and prepared for you, do not be afraid to step into the river for it will part for you. Much preparation has been done in you and in the same wisdom; much has been done in the place that I AM calling you.

So many times you thought I was doing nothing, but the fact remains a great and mighty work has been done unbeknownst to you. I have never forsaken you although you may have thought that I have. Many times I have been carrying you and protecting you and guiding you through areas that you were never aware of, all the while holding you in the palm of my hand.

Beloved, I saw every question, every concern, every tear... Never forsaking you...EVER! I have placed upon each of you a calling like no other. I have placed upon each of your hearts... A hunger and desire to serve ME. An all-consuming desire, consuming your thoughts at this very time passed. Through the times of doubts, loneliness and hardships...times when you have cried out to Me, **"Where are You God?"**

## You promised to move mightily in my life, where are You?

I say to you, here AM I in the midst. Even when you are surrounded by distractions, and the distractions have been many, I AM in your midst. Keep your eyes and your heart focused on Me, do not be moved, for I will move mightily. Many are called but few are chosen and I AM well pleased that you have stood and remain firm in your calling. One word of caution, my daughter, you are serving ME, not man! You have faced opposition in the past and you will face opposition in the future, such is the coarse of one who truly follows Me. Mankind will try to dissuade you—set your face like flint—only following and serving Me.

Over these past days and hours, I have been placing within your spirit, a stirring of hope and a stirring assurance in your heart for the call upon your life. This stirring will begin to bring the flow of MY SPIRIT. You sensed that there is a moving, 'a tangible' moving taking place. Do not denounce it but grasp and lay hold of what I lay before you. The time being held in limbo is now coming to an end for MY SPIRIT is moving in a mighty way!

Give ear to My Word and remember my precepts---they are for instruction and wealth.

Take note of every jot and tittle---they are for a purpose. I do not give words of non-effect or non meanings. Each word to you has been carefully picked for your edification and for your instruction.

Do not discount MY WORDS but take heed and give ear. Weigh them very carefully!

My Beloved Daughter, you have been in a most vulnerable place because it is the place where I AM positioning you to enter and claim your inheritance.

A place where often all you can do is 'stand'. My Daughter, through it all, I AM delighted with your obedience and My recompense and reward is with ME!

My Daughter, I will never allow you, My faithful one to lose or miss your inheritance and blessings. You can be sure ALL that I HAVE PROMISED YOU WILL BE FULFILLED!

Breakthrough, breakthrough, breakthrough...I AM THE BREAKER AND I AM BREAKING THROUGH every door and every hold that would try to bind you. Your LORD GOD ALMIGHTY is doing this thing and I AM BREAKING THROUGH ON YOUR BEHALF!

I AM reaching out My arm to you this day and I say come away MY BELOVED to that secret place reserved only for you. The time is right, the day is here, I AM calling you forth. It is no accident that I have chosen this season to bring release to you and to your calling. It is a new beginning that you are celebrating; a new day and a new hour is dawning. So lift up your eyes, My Daughter and see your Father and your God bring to pass all that I have promised....

**Lift up your eyes for a mighty work has been accomplished.**
**Lift up your eyes to the hills from which cometh your help.**
**Your help cometh from the Lord!**
**Lift up your eyes for the unveiling...**

You will stand in amazement in what I AM unveiling.

You will watch in amazement at the unveiling. I said that I would do it and I AM fulfilling My Word!

You will see that shortly it will be your triumphant day, a day of breakthrough, a day of triumph over all the enemy has tried to do to hold you back. It will be a day of laying forth the plans I have for you and the triumphant entering into these plans. It is a glorious entering in of you with your King!

Listen My Daughter, for the trumpets are sounding and My angels have gone forth.

Get ready for your glorious visitation. Get ready to receive the voice of your God, as the mysteries of My will shall be revealed to you. Do not question MY instructions but move in them. They will bring an excitement to your spirit and music to your ears.

***You will say, "I can't believe it!"***

***"But Beloved, you will believe!"***

Don't believe or settle for the lies of the enemy that would say it's not going to happen. Let the words of My mouth be the final say in your life knowing you can rely on what I say. And know that it is truth and it cannot change or fail!

My Daughter stand on My Word. It is life to you. Stand fast, stand fast and don't let go. Hold fast, stand fast and you will see that I AM bringing into the physical realm those things I have accomplished in the spiritual realm. You will stand in amazement for your thoughts, your conceptions of what I would do, could not even begin to compare to what I AM really doing. You will stand amazed at what I AM bringing forth. The way has been hard and the road has been rough but it is time to rise up o' woman of God! Rise up and take your rightful place. A place only prepared for you! I have been knitting you with like-sisters who have known much heartache, suffering and pain and those who have no need of personal glory. Cherish My precious gift unto you! The hour and the minute is upon you...

**Rise up o' woman of God!**

**Amen.**

## Rise Up O Man of God

The words carry the spirit of the old English hymns written by Charles Wesley and others. The text reads:

***Rise up, O Men of God!***

*Have done with lesser things.*

*Give heart and soul and mind and strength*

*To serve the King of Kings.*

*Rise up, O men of God,*

*In one united throng.*

*Bring in the day of brotherhood*

*And end the night of wrong.*

*Rise up, O men of God!*

*The church for you doth wait,*

*Her strength unequal to her task;*

*Rise up, and make her great!*

*Rise up, O men of God!*

*Tread where his feet have trod.*

*As brothers of the Son of Man,*

*Rise up, O men of God!*

Recently we put a book together titled: **Simply This: The World's Greatest Message**

And of course this message is and always will be: "Jesus Christ is Lord!" There is no other and while not all the world receives it, it is meant for men and women alike. God is no respecter of persons. There is no gender in Heaven and when we go we shall understand this more fully.

This book we wrote was put in our spirit to aim at the new believer and their walk with the Lord. I included 'Rise Up O Woman of God' and never thought about the gender bias I was creating, but wrote about what I knew. But recently I had an urgent question about this and did I have a book for men, obviously they thought our book was for women and rightfully so. That's who we generally minister to. That's who fortunately the churches are full of and its women. Please know I would love to have a men's following but God has not mentioned it to me yet. But I know my husband will be ready when we do. Praise God! There is something stirring in the spirit realm.

Men my thoughts for you are this, Jesus spoke it in red letters in my Bible, so they must be urgent:

1. *Matthew 22:37 Jesus said unto him, Thou shalt love the Lord thy God with all thy heart, and with all thy soul, and with all thy mind.*

2. *Ephesians 5:25 Husbands, love your wives, even as Christ also loved the church, and gave himself for it; 26 That he might sanctify and cleanse it with the washing of water by the word, 27 That he might present it to himself a glorious church, not having spot, or wrinkle, or any such thing; but that it should be holy and without blemish.*

3. *Serve God and trust Him.*

There is so much to say but without being a man, I can only suppose. My Father in Heaven is a spirit and He treats us very well by giving us eternal life and all that goes with it. I had a Dad here on earth and a brother and they have both passed on but my husband is very special to me for many reasons. Please remember that Love triumphs all! God = Love and without love you don't have much.

*1 John 4:8*
*He that loveth not knoweth not God; for God is love.*

This scripture makes it very simple and for me sets it in stone. If you have not love then you have not God. If you have love then you are complete. Rise up o men of God and love one another as God loves you. Be a fine example to others who need your example for their own lives. Love will drive a matter in the right direction. What does the Bible say about us?

*John 13:35*
*By this shall all men know that ye are my disciples, if ye have love one to another.*

If we follow Jesus and we are His disciples and we must love like Jesus loved. He is the boss; He is the example we follow each and every time.

## Let's pray with you:

*Dear Heavenly Father,*
*We pray in Jesus name,*
*Help us to rise up,*
*And be the men and women you have called*
*us to be.*
*Lord we need you today,*
*And we need your strength to stand up,*
*Against doubt and fear,*
*Of whom we are.*
*We are Sons and Daughters of the King.*
*Thank You Lord,*
*Amen.*

# CHAPTER TEN

## Forgiveness is Beautiful

One of the most beautiful things God has given us is forgiveness! Oh my, oh my, it is so priceless and of high value to you and I. Father God sent His Son to the cross to die for our sins so we could be forgiven. Jesus shed His blood so we could be forgiven. How beautiful is that? It took death to give us life again. Now why aren't you forgiving your neighbor, your sister or your best friend again?

There are many types of forgiveness and we have access to them all through Jesus Christ our Lord and Savior. He saved us from our sins but as He walked this earth, He taught us also. He taught us many times about forgiveness. He said love one another as I have loved you.

Go the extra mile to forgive someone. What does the Bible say about going extra, not necessarily about forgiveness but in all things of life:

## Matthew 5:40-42

*40 And if any man will sue thee at the law, and take away thy coat, let him have thy cloak also.*

*41 And whosoever shall compel thee to go a mile, go with him twain.*

*42 Give to him that asketh thee, and from him that would borrow of thee turn not thou away.*

This is beautiful! God has spoken these things to me in my walk with Him and I have studied these scriptures because I think they are important. 40: if man needs your shirt, give him your coat too. 41: If someone asks you to go one mile, go two with them. 42: If someone needs to borrow something, give it to them instead. Mind you, you will be tested in these precepts. I have certainly and the blessing came as I passed the test. I am sure there are some tests yet to pass. But sowing and reaping as we give generously to others, will never get old. This is like forgiveness; it's always available and it's always needed. Who do you need to forgive today?

God has forgiven us in salvation, do you remember? It was a beautiful time. Probably the most beautiful time in anyone's life is the salvation through Jesus Christ our Lord. He forgave all of our sins. There is rarely a book that

I write that the Holy Spirit brings it to my heart to write about it. So it must still be prevalent and a problem on the earth; in the Body of Christ. We know the world cannot forgive the way the believers can forgive, so let's set a good example. Just say:

**"Lord, I forgive them all, in Jesus mighty name!**

Clear your heart of any obstruction today. Let not your heart be troubled and stay faithful to the scriptures that say:

*Matthew 6:14-15*

*14 For if ye forgive men their trespasses, your heavenly Father will also forgive you:*

*15 But if ye forgive not men their trespasses, neither will your Father forgive your trespasses.*

We must forgive, so we can be free to be beautiful as the Lord has called us to be. Unforgiveness ranks high on the sickness and disease charts as the root cause many times. Because unforgiveness turns into a root of bitterness after awhile and it makes your body sick. Ask me, I can tell you all about it. The Lord delivered me several times from the root of bitterness and yet there was more. My root caused colon cancer and I had to have surgery and much prayer. I got delivered by the hand of God but imagine the mess I would have had if I did not listen or do something about it. God moved on me quickly, He knew my history. My Mom died of cancer; my grandfather too. We broke that generational curse too and I forgave all. But the Lord showed me who I was unforgiving with and I had to repent.

The Book of Matthew helps us so much in these beautiful things of forgiveness. Take note here:

*Matthew 18:20-22*

*20 For where two or three are gathered together in my name, there am I in the midst of them.*

*21 Then came Peter to him, and said, Lord, how oft shall my brother sin against me, and I forgive him? till seven times?*

*22 Jesus saith unto him, I say not unto thee, Until seven times: but, Until seventy times seven.*

Forgive at all times, how about that? It is a beautiful thing to do. I often wonder if we will make Heaven with unforgiveness in our hearts?

Somehow I doubt that because in scripture it surely says that if we do not forgive then our Father in Heaven will not forgive us. Wow! Don't keep anything ugly in your heart, forgive and cast your cares upon Jesus and then repent for your actions. Life is too good to mess it up because of what others have done to us. We don't hurt them, we only hurt ourselves and Heaven is waiting for those beautiful things you have to offer others by giving up that mess you have been carrying around. Forgiveness is key to being intimate with the Father. Let's get r' done!

*1 Peter 5:7*
*Casting all your care upon him; for he careth for you.*

**Let's pray with you:**

*Dear Heavenly Father,*
*Forgive us in Jesus name,*
*Please help us to forgive others without regret.*
*Father cleanse our hearts and deliver us.*
*Help us to be all brand new,*
*As we cast all our cares upon Jesus.*
*Thank You Lord,*
*Amen.*

# CHAPTER ELEVEN

## What is More Beautiful Than Love

L-O-V-E is thee most beautiful thing God has given us because GOD is LOVE! He gave us Him! He loves us so much and we should love Him more than any one thing or person. Love is so good!

*Deuteronomy 11:13-14*

*13 And it shall come to pass, if ye shall hearken diligently unto my commandments which I command you this day, to love the LORD your God, and to serve him with all your heart and with all your soul,*

*14 That I will give you the rain of your land in his due season, the first rain and the latter rain, that thou mayest gather in thy corn, and thy wine, and thine oil.*

As I write in Chapter 1-1, (eleven) I think of walking one on one with God. Adam and Eve did it why can't we? The number 11 is like two stick figures walking as one. This is my version, maybe not yours but when I think of 1-1, I know I can do it walking with the Lord. He keeps me in step with Him; He gives angels charge over me and directs my steps. Love is the answer. We wrote a book last year titled: LOVE is Surely The Way by Susan J Perry and so far everyone enjoys it. They love the love book. I loved doing it as the Holy Spirit hovered over me many times as I typed on my computer to get the words and scriptures right. I flow when I write and I try to operate in that sweet love God gives us. I must if I am to teach through these many, many books God has ordained. For some reason He trusts me and that all by itself is beautiful! My heart belongs to Jesus.

Walking one on one with the Lord requires much attention and Bible time devoted to the things of God which I am no expert at but I had given Jesus my heart way back in 1998 and I pray I have never looked back hoping for my old life back. God has shown me beautiful things and love exudes in all He does.

We can talk about beautiful things you say you love: you love your husband; your children; your home; your church, etc... There are many things we say that we love for instance: I love all those and more; I love to write; I love to mow my lawn and I love to go shopping. But that is really not true love is it but only your heart's desire. What is true and abiding love? It is called AGAPE love like God loves us. Let's define this:

•      A simple way to summarize agape is God's perfect, unconditional love.

•      Jesus lived out agape love by sacrificing himself on the cross for the sins of the world.

•      Agape love is more than an emotion. It is a sentiment that demonstrates itself through actions.

•      Selfless love of one person for another without sexual implications (especially love that is spiritual in nature). Agape love is a strong positive emotion of regard and affection; Ex.: His love for his work; children need a lot of love.

Love for me is a great emotional attraction one to another when you forget about yourself and get totally immersed in someone else's life beyond your own needs. It exists and you can have this too. Love that is selfless is so beautiful beyond our wildest dreams. God's love is tangible although many may not think so today; I do because I have felt it. I have known God's love. How about you? Here is the greatest example of God's love I have been able to think of:

*John 3:16*
*For God so loved the world, that he gave his only begotten Son, that whosoever believeth in him should not perish, but have everlasting life.*

This is a picture of the God kind of love. My husband and I went through the Bible stories many are about love but never as generous as the cross was for all of us. This was done so none should perish but have eternal rewards instead. God has put eternity into man's heart so he can come and love Jesus, finally and be saved forever by calling upon his name! This is real love, to love all mankind for eternity. Only God can do this. This is the super-duper kind of love!

**Let us pray with you:**

*Dear Heavenly Father,*
*We come in Jesus name,*
*The name above every name;*
*Thank You for loving me,*
*And taking such good care of me and my family.*
*Blessings dear Father,*
*We love you..*
*Amen.*

# CHAPTER TWELVE

## The Hallmark of Beautiful is Salvation

Our God is so beautiful to offer us free salvation and eternal life through His Son Jesus...

It is all about salvation, each and every day a soul comes to Jesus to stand in the Kingdom of God, there is a celebration in Heaven. Salvation should be everyone's priority right now. This is beyond beautiful in the expanse of Heaven, when one more soul is added to the roles there. Your name added to the Lamb's Book of Life is a time to rejoice for this will have repercussions of eternity.

*Luke 15:10*
*Likewise, I say unto you, there is joy in the presence of the angels of God over one sinner that repenteth.*

As I pondered this next chapter God began speaking to me: *"Beauty for ashes."* I knew this would be my next pertinent scripture and let's see how they pertain here. Beauty/Beautiful is a wonderful thing.

*Isaiah 61:1-3*

*1 The Spirit of the Lord GOD is upon me; because the LORD hath anointed me to preach good tidings unto the meek; he hath sent me to bind up the brokenhearted, to proclaim liberty to the captives, and the opening of the prison to them that are bound;*

*2 To proclaim the acceptable year of the LORD, and the day of vengeance of our God; to comfort all that mourn;*

*3 To appoint unto them that mourn in Zion, to give unto them beauty for ashes, the oil of joy for mourning, the garment of praise for the spirit of heaviness; that they might be called trees of righteousness, the planting of the LORD, that he might be glorified.*

These three scriptures from the Book of Isaiah are some of my favorite beautiful things. Let's break these verses down to see ALL that God wants to say here in this book:

1.  The precious and beautiful Spirit of the Living God is upon me.

2. God has anointed me to tell you the good news of the gospel

3. Speak to the meek; the broken-hearted and proclaim liberty over them because they are bound-up in their own prison;

4. Tell them that this is the acceptable year of the Lord and He will deliver them; revenge their enemies and comfort those who have lost loved ones in this process.

5. All those that mourn in the church still, God will give them an exchange: beauty for ashes and joy for your mourning.

   **JOY COMES>>>MOURNING GO!**

6. God will give you the garment of praise for the spirit of heaviness and you will become trees of righteousness again because the Lord will plant you and He will be glorified.
   *Amen.*

This is the day of salvation and I want you to know its going to be beautiful, exciting and fully charged from on High because God is excited about having you near Him.

*Isaiah 49:8*
*Thus saith the LORD, In an acceptable time have
I heard thee, and in a day of salvation have I
helped thee: and I will preserve thee, and give
thee for a covenant of the people, to establish
the earth, to cause to inherit the desolate
heritages;*

We are the inheritance of the Most High God and He is giving us salvation. We are free to be beautiful in our worship of the Lord. He has made everything beautiful in His time.

We as the children of God are always contending for our families' salvation in prayer. This is a burden we take on as we love our children and our children's children; we are concerned where they will spend eternity. We hope and pray they are concerned too. Here is a scripture I stand on in faith coming out of one of my favorite Books of the Bible:

*Isaiah 49:25*
*But thus saith the LORD, Even the captives of the
mighty shall be taken away, and the prey of the
terrible shall be delivered: for I will contend
with him that contendeth with thee, and I
will save thy children.*

There are three promises that keep me at peace in this scripture:

1. That God will contend with those who contend with me. (to strive against or oppose)

2. That God will save our children (He will give them salvation).

3. The Lord will deliver the prey of the terrible; those held captive He will be set free.

Although this scripture is heavy duty it has some beautiful promises to it. We love God and He keeps His promises to us. His Word is His bond to us and He will never lead anyone astray. Standing on the promises of God are like a solid rock foundation and you must believe to receive. Our lives are made more beautiful through His beautiful Word as we grow in Him each and every day. We can rest assured that these promises are true. Because God gives us peace in every situation, we can know that we know.

*John 14:27*
*Peace I leave with you,*
*my peace I give unto you: not as the*
*world giveth, give I unto you. Let not your*
*heart be troubled, neither let it be afraid.*

God supplied all of our needs for generations to come. This is another favorite verse because Jesus gave us His peace and He is the Prince of Peace. There is no better peace to be found. The world ain't got it and the world can't take it away. Check out how beautiful God is here in this scripture:

*Psalm 105:8*
*He hath remembered his covenant for ever, the word which he commanded to a thousand generations.*

This is really one of those beautiful things: God remembers his covenant and commands (not offered) the word to a ***thousand*** generations. Whoopee!! My generations can go forth or those behind me can live in God's covenant. I love the number one thousand, and I believe this is the largest number in the Bible. So I love God's big beautiful numbers too because why not believe for the BIG from God as well as the small. God has it all. My husband John always says, *"I am going to pray the BIG prayer,"* and I agree with him. On our tithes we always stand on another scripture and it is:

*Deuteronomy 1:11*
*(The LORD God of your fathers make you a thousand times so many more as ye are, and bless you, as he hath promised you!)*

We love those thousand numbers because they are big and grandiose, "NO!" But because they are God's numbers and have given them to us as believers to stand on. Why not go for the biggest and the bestest God has to offer!

Here is another good 'one thousand' scripture with a promise in it:

*Joshua 23:10*
*One man of you shall chase a thousand: for the LORD your God, he it is that fighteth for you, as he hath promised you.*

Amen, I will take this as God fights our battles for us. Joshua was a great example of this. How beautiful can this be? God is a warrior for His children. There is no battle God cannot win. He defeated the devil in the resurrection of Jesus Christ and gave us eternal life with Him. What's better than that?

**Let's pray with you:**

*Dear Heavenly Father,*
*As we come to pray in Jesus name,*
*We thank you for salvation.*
*For saving our families and,*
*For saving our generations;*
*We are standing on your promises in your*
*name,*
*Amen.*

# CHAPTER THIRTEEN

## America the Beautiful

There are songs written about her; declarations signed about her and this is the land we live in today and so thankful for it. Are we standing with her right now? Are we praying for her deliverance; 2021 is the year of 'Great Deliverance' and surely we all need it. How are we handling such a perilous time going on in our land of the free and home of the brave. She is one of God's beautiful things and He has allowed some to live here and prosper here but right now she is in a big battle to keep freedom real for ALL.

"In God We Trust." God is beautiful, but what happens with those who have turned something very beautiful into something so ugly for their grievous benefit, to harm others and eliminate all that this country has been based on for 245 years now as we celebrated this 4th of July in 2021 as our Independence Day. Is this what we have come home to? Our hearts are heavy laden today because of what has been going on in the government of our country where the core is now rotten with corruption and greed. Although we have much seed in the ground of America, we will not be deterred. But to what effect is our seed when the enemy of our souls has illegitimately come in and taken over our country? This is NOT beautiful in any way, shape or form. But the Lord has given us as believers; as the King's kids to take authority in the pulling down of these demonic strongholds. We must be effective today!

*2 Corinthians 10:4*
*(For the weapons of our warfare are not carnal, but mighty through God to the pulling down of strong holds;)*

Look how generous our God is, and how much beauty He has given us; have you ever traveled in America? They call it the 'Land of Opportunity' and many other good things; God has been gracious unto us. Many people from other foreign lands hope to migrate to America to have what we have. There is no other nation with that banner flying high above them with freedom as their inscription. When I see an American flag flying high above me, I can look up knowing it is a beautiful reminder that our country was born free and will remain free even if we have o fight over it. Our country was born:

*"One nation under God, indivisible with liberty and justice for all."*

*Psalm 33:12*
*Blessed is the nation whose God is the LORD; and the people whom he hath chosen for his own*

Has not America chosen God as the Head of our nation? We have it decreed in our legal documents and branded on our money: *"In God We Trust."*

There are so many people today trying to make our country something that it is NOT! We were founded on these good principles and now every good thing, such as in the time of Sodom and Gomorrah is trying to be destroyed in the name of evil. But there are still some of us who pray and believe God for these good things to return to our country instead of the evil that only looks like it is prevailing right now. Like I said it only looks that way right now. The left-wing hate mongers cannot have our beautiful country. America needs this Psalm coming out of its mouth:

*Psalm 80:3*
*Turn us again, O God, and cause thy face to shine; and we shall be saved.*

## *"America will be saved in Jesus name!"*

## Let's pray with you:

*Dear Heavenly Father,*
*We ask you to make America beautiful again,*
*As the songs are said, and the words spoken.*
*As only YOU can do,*
*In Jesus mighty name.*
*Help turn her towards you so she shall prosper.*
*Lord this is your dwelling place,*
*"One Nation Under God!"*
*Keep her as only unto Yourself.*
*In God We Trust,*
*Amen.*

# CHAPTER FOURTEEN

## Peace Like a River

The SAR Shalom of God ~ I woke up this morning and the Lord spoke this chapter to my spirit as soon as I saw light. And I thought another book? No it must be another chapter because peace is such a beautiful thing God gives us. We mentioned it back a few chapters as in chapter 12 as peace that Jesus gives us. Here is the scripture; I am going to repeat it:

*John 14:27*
*Peace I leave with you, my peace I give unto you: not as the world giveth, give I unto you. Let not your heart be troubled, neither let it be afraid.*

There is nothing like God's peace that He gives us, in fact one of the names of Jesus is: The Prince of Peace:

*Isaiah 9:6*
*For unto us a child is born, unto us a son is given: and the government shall be upon his*

*shoulder: and his name shall be called Wonderful, Counsellor, The mighty God, The everlasting Father, The Prince of Peace.*

We are honoring God by taking on His peace. Have you talked to folks today? They do not know peace. Before I knew Jesus I did not know peace. But upon salvation God began to give me peace (fruit of the Spirit) and today I have that blessed assurance. My husband and I live a very peaceable existence thanks to our Lord. It is peace like a river. Many times I have jumped in God's spiritual river to write these books; these God-ideas, just as He spoke to me this morning. There is such a free-flow in God's river and peace has a gentle pace. There is no friction or tumult and it is a safe place, a beautiful thing in God's creation. Let us define the word peace:

**Peace**
/pēs/
**Noun**
  1. freedom from disturbance; tranquility: "You can while away an hour or two in peace and seclusion in peace and seclusion." Similar: tranquility, calm, calmness, restfulness: Opposite: noise or irritation.
  2. a state or period in which there is no war or a war has ended: "The Straits were to be open to warships in time of peace" Similar:

law and order, lawfulness, order, peacefulness. Opposite: conflict.

We have freedom when we are at peace and tranquil. Our lives are calm, cool and collected when we are at peace. Without conflict, there is no fighting while at peace otherwise peace ends as we know it. Are you living this life? Can you be classified as a peaceful person? Are you living in a no-drama zone yet? Some folks exist well in drama and I definitely do not. Peace is like a river flowing, flowing beautifully along. Others witness this life you have and wonder where you get such a peace. We get it from the Prince of Peace, the SAR Shalom of God is in this house, catch the wave in the river as it comes by you now...

**Peace scriptures:**

*Exodus 14:14*
*The LORD shall fight for you, and ye shall hold your peace.*

*Deuteronomy 20:10*
*When thou comest nigh unto a city to fight against it, then proclaim peace unto it.*

*Psalm 29:11*
*The LORD will give strength unto his people; the LORD will bless his people with peace*

**Isaiah 66:12**
**For thus saith the LORD, Behold, I will**
**extend peace to her like a river, and the**
**glory of the Gentiles like a flowing**
**stream: then shall ye suck, ye shall be**
**borne upon her sides, and be dandled**
**upon her knees.**

*Jeremiah 29:11*
*For I know the thoughts that I think toward*
*you, saith the LORD, thoughts of peace, and not*
*of evil, to give you an expected end*

*Jeremiah 33:6*
*Behold, I will bring it health and cure, and I will*
*cure them, and will reveal unto them the*
*abundance of peace and truth*

*John 16:33*
*These things I have spoken unto you, that in me*
*ye might have peace. In the world ye shall have*
*tribulation: but be of good cheer; I have*
*overcome the world.*

*Galatians 5:22-23*

*22 But the fruit of the Spirit is love, joy, peace,*
*longsuffering, gentleness, goodness, faith,*

*23 Meekness, temperance: against such there is*
*no law.*

*Philippians 4:7*
*And the peace of God, which passeth all*
*understanding, shall keep your hearts and*
*minds through Christ Jesus.*

Jump into the river of God with peace as your guide; peace like a river! It flows and flows as God gives us peace... (See Isaiah 66:12 highlighted above). Here is more in the Psalm of David:

*Psalm 46:1-4*

*1 God is our refuge and strength, a very present help in trouble.*

*2 Therefore will not we fear, though the earth be removed, and though the mountains be carried into the midst of the sea;*

*3 Though the waters thereof roar and be troubled, though the mountains shake with the swelling thereof. Selah.*

*4 There is a river, the streams whereof shall make glad the city of God, the holy place of the tabernacles of the most High.*

God gives us peace no matter how our life's journey is going whether in a rollercoaster or a tumultuous sea; He will give you His peace like no other possibly can. This is definitely, without any question one of the most beautiful things that only He can give us. Let us celebrate the peace of God!

And just one more thought on peace: What did Jesus say on the Sermon on the Mount when He taught the Beatitudes to the multitudes?

*Matthew 5:9*
*Blessed are the peacemakers: for they shall be called the children of God.*

We shall be called the children of God. What more appropriate status can you have with God as you stay peaceful in the Family of God? Be known as a peacemaker instead of a trouble maker or rabble-rouser but wait on the Lord and be of good courage: Peace is on the way. Study all of Chapter 5 of Matthew. This is beautiful!

**Let's pray with you:**

*Dear Heavenly Father,*
*We come in the name of Jesus;*
*And we thank You for the Prince of Peace,*
*Who gives us this peace that is beyond understanding.*
*Thank You for speaking to,*
*Our tumultuous seas this day,*
*Amen.*

# CHAPTER FIFTEEN

## Honor is Beautiful

With all honour, the KJV pretty much spells it with the 'u' in it. The Americans spell it 'honor' and the English add a 'u' as in 'honour.' We must go with the scriptural accreditation of the word. They have done the same with favor and favour. They mean the same but a 'u' is added for flavor I suppose.

Honoring someone is a beautiful thing that God does or appoints someone else to do. When you are an honorable person, you sow honor and reap honor. Let us define this word:

**Honor**
hon·or | \ ˈä-nər \
**Noun**
*Definition of* honor
(Entry 1 of 2)
   1. good name or public esteem: Reputation
      a) a showing of usually merited respect: Recognition: pay *honor* to our founder

2. Privilege: had the *honor* of joining the captain for dinner
3. a person of superior standing —now used especially as a title for a holder of high office: if Your *Honor* please
4. one whose worth brings respect or fame: Credit an *honor* to the profession
5. the center point of the upper half of an armorial escutcheon
6. an evidence or symbol of distinction:
     a) such as an exalted title or rank
     b) BADGE, DECORATION
          1) a ceremonial rite or observance; buried with full military *honors*
     c) an award in a contest or field of competition
     d) *archaic*: a gesture of deference: bow
     e) honors *plural*
          1) an academic distinction conferred on a superior student
          2) a course of study for superior students supplementing or replacing a regular course
7. Chastity, Purity fought fiercely for her *honor* and her life
8. a keen sense of ethical conduct: Integrity a man of *honor*

a) one's word given as a guarantee of performance on my *honor*, I will be there
9. honors *plural*: social courtesies or civilities extended by a host asked her to do the *honors*.
10. an ace, king, queen, jack, or ten especially of the trump suit in bridge
    a) the scoring value of honors held in bridge —usually used in plural
    b) the privilege of playing first from the tee in golf

## Honor

hon·or | \ ˈä-nər \
honored; honoring\ ˈä-nə-riŋ , ˈän-riŋ \
Verb
Definition of *honor* (Entry 2 of 2)
transitive verb
1. to regard or treat (someone) with admiration and respect: to regard or treat with honor
    a. to give special recognition to: to confer honor on
2. to live up to or fulfill the terms of honor a commitment
    a) to accept as payment honor a credit card
3. to salute with a bow in square dancing

According to the world's dictionaries there are many types of honor and this gives you a small microcosm of what they think. My honor eyes are focused on God and His people and how we must honor them today. Honor is a very beautiful thing created by God. Let's go to scripture in both spellings and touch on the Psalms and on Proverbs; that is a big enough field to plow and this word honor has 178 verses attached to it otherwise. Let's stick with wisdom verses about honor:

*Psalm 7:5*
*Let the enemy persecute my soul, and take it; yea, let him tread down my life upon the earth, and lay mine honour in the dust. Selah.*

*Psalm 8:5*
*For thou hast made him a little lower than the angels, and hast crowned him with glory and honour. (man)*

*Psalm 15:4*
*In whose eyes a vile person is contemned; but he honoureth them that fear the LORD. He that sweareth to his own hurt, and changeth not.*

*Psalm 21:5*
*His glory is great in thy salvation: honour and majesty hast thou laid upon him.*

*Psalm 26:8*
*L*ORD*, I have loved the habitation of thy house,*
*and the place where thine honour dwelleth.*

*Psalm 45:9*
*Kings' daughters were among thy honourable*
*women: upon thy right hand did stand the*
*queen in gold of Ophir.*

*Psalm 49:12*
*Nevertheless man being in honour abideth not:*
*he is like the beasts that perish.*

*Psalm 91:15*
*He shall call upon me, and I will answer him: I*
*will be with him in trouble; I will deliver him,*
*and honour him.*

*Psalm 104:1*
*Bless the L*ORD*, O my soul. O L*ORD *my God, thou*
*art very great; thou art clothed*
*with honour and majesty.*

*Psalm 112:9*
*He hath dispersed, he hath given to the poor;*
*his righteousness endureth for ever; his horn*
*shall be exalted with honour.*

*Psalm 145:5*
*I will speak of the glorious honour of thy*
*majesty, and of thy wondrous works.*

*Psalm 149:9*
*To execute upon them the judgment written:*
*this honour have all his saints. Praise ye*
*the LORD.*

*Proverbs 3:9*
*Honour the LORD with thy substance, and with*
*the firstfruits of all thine increase:*

*Proverbs 3:16*
*Length of days is in her right hand; and in her*
*left hand riches and honour.*

*Proverbs 4:8*
*Exalt her, and she shall promote thee: she shall*
*bring thee to honour, when thou dost*
*embrace her.*

*Proverbs 8:18*
*Riches and honour are with me; yea, durable*
*riches and righteousness.*

*Proverbs 11:16*
*A gracious woman retaineth honour: and*
*strong men retain riches.*

*Proverbs 15:33*
*The fear of the LORD is the instruction of*
*wisdom; and before honour is humility.*

*Proverbs 21:21*
*He that followeth after righteousness and*
*mercy findeth life, righteousness, and honour.*

*Proverbs 22:4*
*By humility and the fear of the* Lord *are riches,*
*and honour, and life.*

*Proverbs 25:2*
*It is the glory of God to conceal a thing: but*
*the honour of kings is to search out a matter.*

*Proverbs 26:1*
*As snow in summer, and as rain in harvest,*
*so honour is not seemly for a fool.*

*Proverbs 29:23*
*A man's pride shall bring him low:*
*but honour shall uphold the humble in spirit.*

*A Proverbs 31 Woman:*

*Proverbs 31:25*
*Strength and honour are her clothing; and she*
*shall rejoice in time to come.*

By reading theses scriptures, you see and
understand there is great substance with God in
honour. We often pray Lord, I praise you and
honour you and glorify your name. Honour is a
high-ranking substance with our God in Heaven

because He is honorable; faithful and loving in every way about Him and so should we be. If you cannot be honorable with someone, I believe it's better to walk away from them than to dishonor them. We stand in honor with God this way. This is a beautiful thing, to be in right-standing with God. Stay honorable and God will honor you. Hallelujah!

# CHAPTER SIXTEEN

## Repentance is Beautiful

A heart must be ready to meet with Jesus and after all He is the way, the truth and the life. I have always heard others say that He would make a way where there doesn't seem to be a way. I always pictured God blowing a hole in the wall of the building so I could go through; or taking a bull-dozer and creating a new path in the ground through a thick forest in those impossible spots that you could never get through yourself. He could make a special road just for you and me. That is exactly what repentance does for you. It makes a way for Jesus to come into your heart and make you brand new. This is real beauty. Let's define repentance right here and now:

## Repentance:

Repentance is the activity of reviewing one's actions and feeling contrition or regret for past wrongs, which is accompanied by commitment to and actual actions that show and prove a change for the better. In modern times, it is generally seen as involving a commitment to personal change and the resolve to live a more responsible and humane life; in other words, being sorry for one's misdeeds. (Wikipedia)

Re·pent·ance
/rəˈpentəns/
*Noun*
1. the action of repenting; sincere regret or remorse: "each person who turns to God in genuine repentance and faith will be saved"

For me it's going to the altar of God and confessing all your sins at His Throne of Grace. God will always welcome you. Some times we go to these altars in our prayer-time too, privately before God.

*Hebrews 4:16*
*Let us therefore come boldly unto*
*the throne of grace, that we may obtain mercy,*
*and find grace to help in time of need*

Here the Lord will cleanse you and make you beautiful inside and out to come before His holy throne. He is a holy God who loves you and wants you in His Kingdom for the duration of time spent on earth and in heaven, and then forever.

Learning to live and love in God's Kingdom is an extreme honor and a most beautiful thing; at least it certainly has been for me. Repentance draws us near to the heart of God. Let's do some scriptures on repentance and I'm sure a clearer picture will come forth. Both John the Baptist and Jesus repeated the same message in the New Testament, in the Book of Matthew:

*Matthew 3:1-3*

*1 In those days came John the Baptist, preaching in the wilderness of Judea,*

*2 And saying, Repent ye: for the kingdom of heaven is at hand.*

*3 For this is he that was spoken of by the prophet Esaias, saying, The voice of one crying in the wilderness, Prepare ye the way of the Lord, make his paths straight.*

Jesus came upon the scene and repeated John the Baptist's words because to repent is very important in the Kingdom of God and truth.

*Matthew 4:15-17*

*15 The land of Zabulon, and the land of Nephthalim, by the way of the sea, beyond Jordan, Galilee of the Gentiles;*

*16 The people which sat in darkness saw great light; and to them which sat in the region and shadow of death light is sprung up.*

*17 From that time Jesus began to preach, and to say, Repent: for the kingdom of heaven is at hand.*

Jesus speaks again saying:

*Matthew 9:13*
*But go ye and learn what that meaneth, I will have mercy, and not sacrifice: for I am not come to call the righteous, but sinners to repentance.*

We are all sinners at birth until we come into the Kingdom of God and repent and receive Jesus in our hearts. Let's do that today, right here and right now. Here is a sinner's prayer:

**Today is the Day of salvation...**

*2 Corinthians 6:2*
*(For he saith, I have heard thee in a time accepted, and in the day of salvation have I succoured thee: behold, now is the accepted time; behold, now is the day of salvation.)*

## Don't miss out... Pray with me!

*Dear Heavenly Father,*
*I receive Jesus in my heart and draw close to*
*You today.*
*I want to know You more,*
*Please forgive my sins, I repent of this life,*
*I have led without you.*
*Come and give me the light of your salvation;*
*Be my Lord and Savior.*
*I believe Jesus was born to save me;*
*Died to forgive my sin and*
*Resurrected to give His life as a sacrifice for me,*
*Please Lord show me the way today...*
*Amen.*

Now please get a Bible and read it daily. Pray to Jesus every day as well and find a good Bible-based church and tell them you are a new believer and they will help you. Don't let time pass you by. You could miss so much!

This is such a beautiful life as you have given it unto the Lord. Stay repentant and beauty will live in you as the Lord will guide you in every step you take from now on. You will have His protection and love for all eternity.

# CHAPTER SEVENTEEN

## Family is a Beautiful Thing

God created man and then woman on the sixth day...

*Genesis 1:26-28, 31*

*26 And God said, Let us make man in our image, after our likeness: and let them have dominion over the fish of the sea, and over the fowl of the air, and over the cattle, and over all the earth, and over every creeping thing that creepeth upon the earth.*

*27 So God created man in his own image, in the image of God created he him; male and female created he them.*

*28 And God blessed them, and God said unto them, Be fruitful, and multiply, and replenish the earth, and subdue it: and have dominion over the fish of the sea, and over the fowl of the air, and over every living thing that moveth upon the earth.*

*31 And God saw every thing that he had made, and, behold, it was very good. And the evening and the morning were the sixth day.*

*It was all good!*

*Genesis 2:7-10*

*7 And the LORD God formed man of the dust of the ground, and breathed into his nostrils the breath of life; and man became a living soul.*

*8 And the LORD God planted a garden eastward in Eden; and there he put the man whom he had formed.*

*9 And out of the ground made the LORD God to grow every tree that is pleasant to the sight, and good for food; the tree of life also in the midst of the garden, and the tree of knowledge of good and evil.*

*10 And a river went out of Eden to water the garden; and from thence it was parted, and became into four heads.*

God creates man to live in a garden:

*11 The name of the first is Pison: that is it which compasseth the whole land of Havilah, where there is gold;*

*12 And the gold of that land is good: there is bdellium and the onyx stone.*

*13 And the name of the second river is Gihon: the same is it that compasseth the whole land of Ethiopia.*

*14 And the name of the third river is Hiddekel: that is it which goeth toward the east of Assyria. And the fourth river is Euphrates.*

*15 And the LORD God took the man, and put him into the garden of Eden to dress it and to keep it.*

God gave man his first job, caring for the garden. Now his second job was given:

*Genesis 2:16-19*

*16 And the LORD God commanded the man, saying, Of every tree of the garden thou mayest freely eat:*

*17 But of the tree of the knowledge of good and evil, thou shalt not eat of it: for in the day that thou eatest thereof thou shalt surely die.*

*18 And the LORD God said, It is not good that the man should be alone; I will make him an help meet for him.*

*19 And out of the ground the LORD God formed every beast of the field, and every fowl of the air; and brought them unto Adam to see what he would call them: and whatsoever Adam called every living creature, that was the name thereof.*

God decides it is not good for man to be alone in the garden although there is much work to do but needs something more as in verse 18. God creates wo-man. But first Adam must name all the animals himself.

*Genesis 2:20-25*

*20 And Adam gave names to all cattle, and to the fowl of the air, and to every beast of the field; but for Adam there was not found an help meet for him.*

*21 And the LORD God caused a deep sleep to fall upon Adam, and he slept: and he took one of his ribs, and closed up the flesh instead thereof;*

*22 And the rib, which the LORD God had taken from man, made he a woman, and brought her unto the man.*

*23 And Adam said, This is now bone of my bones, and flesh of my flesh: she shall be called Woman, because she was taken out of Man.*

*24 Therefore shall a man leave his father and his mother, and shall cleave unto his wife: and they shall be one flesh.*

*25 And they were both naked, the man and his wife, and were not ashamed.*

This is how God created the first family, a beautiful thing. And today do we even acknowledge this fact as we go forward? God took a long look into what He must create as the family took formation. He gave them a place to live; He gave them provision and He gave them a mate to go forth and multiply bring the family closer together as it grew. He gave them animals to care for and a lawn to mow; food to eat and very pleasant surrounding as they went forth to multiply and grow in this very famous garden. This is a picture-perfect beautiful thing.

In all of this perfection sin came in the garden to beguile the man and the woman of Adam and Eve leading them to destruction.

## Genesis 3:1-7

*1 Now the serpent was more subtil than any beast of the field which the LORD God had made. And he said unto the woman, Yea, hath God said, Ye shall not eat of every tree of the garden?*

*2 And the woman said unto the serpent, We may eat of the fruit of the trees of the garden:*

*3 But of the fruit of the tree which is in the midst of the garden, God hath said, Ye shall not eat of it, neither shall ye touch it, lest ye die.*

*4 And the serpent said unto the woman, Ye shall not surely die:*

*5 For God doth know that in the day ye eat thereof, then your eyes shall be opened, and ye shall be as gods, knowing good and evil.*

*6 And when the woman saw that the tree was good for food, and that it was pleasant to the eyes, and a tree to be desired to make one wise, she took of the fruit thereof, and did eat, and gave also unto her husband with her; and he did eat.*

*7 And the eyes of them both were opened, and they knew that they were naked; and they sewed fig leaves together, and made themselves aprons.*

Here is where the devil introduced man to sin and all that God created was tainted concerning man. There was now sin in the camp. I am not convinced that this was all part of God's plan. The Bible says there's nothing that happens that the Lord does not know about. He had a plan for sin and it was Jesus Christ but man had to go through much tribulation to get there. I thank God I am in the Jesus Christ era and not the sacrifice of animals upon the altars. Because I too am imperfect until God takes me home to perfect me.

I have a family, my husband has a family and together we have the family of God as our church family or the Body of Christ. God created us as His family although we do not always resemble Him. He is so beautiful! He allows us these benefits of being His family. We can bicker and argue, dislike someone but you are going to forgive them and move on. They will still be family. The same with your immediate family, we are blood related. We love them no matter what. With Jesus Christ we are blood family. I feel very assured that we carry the blood DNA of Christ when we accept Him in salvation. We are family and He gives us an inheritance and it is Eternal Life. How can we deny this because Jesus died so we could live eternally with Him. He is family; the Head of our family and we must love one another as He loves us. Love is real important because love is God; He is love. How can you claim to love your family if you do not love and cherish God the Father; God the Son and God the Holy Spirit? We must serve the Most High. Jesus has the heart of a servant as He washed the feet of His disciples at Passover time as He knew the Cross was imminently before Him. Love was guiding Him all the way to the Cross. This is real family, a truer one ever known of man is that of Jesus Christ. This is a beautiful thing!

## Let's pray with you:

*Dear Heavenly Father,*
*We bring this beauty to you,*
*Your child in the family of God.*
*Give them peace and the love they need.*
*Thank You Lord for all You do,*
*To sustain this family,*
*In Jesus name,*
*Amen.*

# CHAPTER EIGHTEEN

## Trusting God is Beautiful

Do you trust God today? Does He trust you? Trust is such a beautiful thing as it helps us to grow in the Lord.

Remember as a kid your Mom sent you on a babysitting job, because she trusted you? She sent you to the neighborhood store with money and a list to buy a few things for the house because she trusted you? Do you remember the first time you realized you were serving God in some way and all of a sudden it dawned on you that He, God Almighty trusted you? Wow that was an eye-opening moment for me and heart-rending too. "GOD TRUSTS ME?"

You could have blown me over with a feather in that moment and I would have fallen over immediately. But I was single, in the middle of my bed praying and seeking God (I can still see it today as I remember) and suddenly I realized God trusted me. It was an eye-opening moment and I was overwhelmed. I cried and cried knowing this was the Lord speaking to my heart, little ole me, so I could write about this over 20 years later in this beautiful book. What a beautiful memory too! I was amazed! I was overwhelmed and I knew that I knew that God loved and trusted me. I knew He would demonstrate this to me in many ways in the days to come. Did I know how? No but He trusted me and now I had to show Him as He showed me the way. He directed the steps of my feet.

How beautiful it is when someone trusts you? It is a safe feeling that you can walk out on the branch of a tree and never fall and break your neck. We have one book titled: ASK for WISDOM: The Safe Harbor of God. Trust is like that because in God He protects us even when we mess up and we will mess up but God's trust is eternal and now we have a big space in time to repent and get back into God's good graces. Not make a fool of Him but continue in the fear of the Lord with respect and trust. Here are some scriptures that offer wisdom in trust in the Book of Proverbs:

*Proverbs 3:5-6*

*5 Trust in the LORD with all thine heart; and lean not unto thine own understanding.*

*6 In all thy ways acknowledge him, and he shall
direct thy paths*

*Proverbs 11:28*
*He that trusteth in his riches shall fall; but the
righteous shall flourish as a branch.*

*Proverbs 16:20*
*He that handleth a matter wisely shall find
good: and whoso trusteth in the LORD, happy
is he.*

*Proverbs 22:19*
*That thy trust may be in the LORD, I have made
known to thee this day, even to thee.*

*Proverbs 28:25*
*He that is of a proud heart stirreth up strife: but
he that putteth his trust in the LORD shall be
made fat.*

*Proverbs 28:26*
*He that trusteth in his own heart is a fool: but
whoso walketh wisely, he shall be delivered.*

*Proverbs 29:25*
*The fear of man bringeth a snare: but whoso
putteth his trust in the LORD shall be safe.*

*Proverbs 30:5*
*Every word of God is pure: he is a shield unto*
*them that put their trust in him.*


*Proverbs 31:11*
*The heart of her husband doth safely trust in*
*her, so that he shall have no need of spoil.*


Proverbs spoke to us here, trusting in the Lord
is such a beautiful thing and comes with many
benefits from Heaven and those around you.
When my husband and I were first married as
we went to church together we took many
classes after church hours to study the Word.
Our first class together was Proverbs and we
studied for a year and the minister got in trouble
at this church for taking so long on one subject.
It was life-changing for us and the wisdom of
Proverbs has permeated our lives. Here is
another example of how God trusts us in the
Book of Ephesians:

*Ephesians 1:9-14*


*9 Having made known unto us the mystery of*
*his will, according to his good pleasure which*
*he hath purposed in himself:*

*10 That in the dispensation of the fulness of*
*times he might gather together in one all things*

*in Christ, both which are in heaven, and which*
*are on earth; even in him:*

*11 In whom also we have obtained an*
*inheritance, being predestinated according to*
*the purpose of him who worketh all things after*
*the counsel of his own will:*

*12 That we should be to the praise of his glory,*
*who first trusted in Christ.*

*13 In whom ye also trusted, after that ye heard*
*the word of truth, the gospel of your salvation:*
*in whom also after that ye believed, ye were*
*sealed with that holy Spirit of promise,*

*14 Which is the earnest of our inheritance until*
*the redemption of the purchased possession,*
*unto the praise of his glory.*

God has given us an inheritance in Christ
Jesus; we are alive because of Him and we have
His promises as well because He trusts us. We
are in Jesus, He can be trusted not our human
flesh but by the Spirit; in the Spirit we have
trust. These scriptures from Ephesians are fresh
and new to this book, and this is definitely a
beautiful thing like a breath of fresh air! Breathe
in the Word of God and get an all-new
perspective.

## Let's pray with you:

*Dear Heavenly Father,*
*Bless this reader and teach all,*
*To trust you my Lord,*
*For there is none like you,*
*In Jesus mighty name,*
*Amen.*

# CHAPTER NINETEEN

## Mentorship is Beautiful

God is just showing me mentorship is so beautiful in the Body of Christ; friendship and the love of God develops in this area of mentoring one. Who is the lover of our soul any way? Jesus sees to our soul as we mature in Christ when we should be helping others find their way. Let's define mentor:

Men·tor
/ˈmenˌtôr/
*Noun*
1. an experienced and trusted adviser: "he was her friend and mentor until his death in 1915"

*Verb*
1. advise or train (someone, especially a younger colleague):"both trainees were expertly mentored by a site supervisor"

I really like this definition: A trusted adviser. Are you helping anyone in the Body grow in the Lord? I suppose it must be time as others have helped us. We must repay this kindness in building the Kingdom of God. Some just do not understand. They pray, they believe but yet their understanding is hindered in some way. Now it's your time to grow and mentor someone else. This is even a new possibility for me as we have one lady in church that is struggling day to day, with some needs of mentoring. Let's see if we can help. How about you? Do you ever neglect the help of others in need? We must find the time to share what has been given to us to those around us. It may be a young child or a full grown person depending on God's direction of course.

Many need help in the Body of Christ. We must discern the body; some are very tight lipped because they have been so hurt before. Mentorship is a beautiful thing when we help one of God's children to grow and mature in Him so they won't give up or fall away. How can we fall away from the Love of God? Many do and Jesus went after the one sheep and left the ninety-nine behind to save that one. We need help some times and many are fearful of asking for that help. But we all know who they are in the Body. I bet you could point out one in your own congregation, easily. Discerning the body and the issues it carries with them; some times it is just a good understanding that is lacking.

Friendship with others in the Body of Christ is valuable because your world changed through salvation; through mentorship we can grow and learn. There are some things we cannot tell everybody because they are personal and not everyone can respect your life as you think they should. Be very careful who you speak your things to because some folks cannot handle where you are going. Not all will go with you. Promotion comes from God; try to grow with a very unique type of person; a sister or a brother in Christ. This terminology is used kind of loosely in the church today but you know the one who takes that seriously and the one you can actually trust. Be very careful. If you are a woman, stay with a woman and if you are a man, stay with a man meaning no opposite friends to befriend in spiritual mentorship. We learned that early on and then there is little temptation involved. Mentorship or counseling should be a safe place. Here is the scripture in Titus to help guide us. This is a beautiful thing!

*Titus 2:3-5*

*3 The aged women likewise, that they be in behaviour as becometh holiness, not false accusers, not given to much wine, teachers of good things;*

*4 That they may teach the young women to be sober, to love their husbands, to love their children,*

*5 To be discreet, chaste, keepers at home, good, obedient to their own husbands, that the word of God be not blasphemed.*

## Let's pray with you:

*Dear Heavenly Father,*
*Help me to mentor others,*
*Help me to be an example of your light.*
*Let my love for you shine through,*
*And help others.*
*Thank you Lord for your gentle guidance,*
*And love.*
*In Jesus name,*
*Amen.*

# CHAPTER TWENTY

## Prosperity is Beautiful

The abundant life; the Zoë life is what the Lord spoke to me about this morning. He wants me to tell you how good it is. It always starts in John 10:10:

*The thief cometh not, but for to steal, and to kill, and to destroy: I am come that they might have life, and that they might have it more abundantly.*

What does abundant really mean according to God's purposes? Let me try to give you the beautiful approach to prosperity. Let's define them all first:

1. **Abundance**
   a) an ample quantity; an abundant amount, PROFUSION a city that has an abundance of fine restaurants
   b) AFFLUENCE, WEALTH; a life of *abundance*
   c) relative degree of plentifulness.

2. **Prosperity**
   a) the state of being successful usually by making a lot of money; a period of *prosperity* for our nation; economic *prosperity*
   b) Biblical prosperity is simple. Biblical prosperity means being blessed by God. God wants you to prosper but He does not necessarily want you financially rich today. If some Christians became financially rich today, it would destroy their true riches (spiritual riches) if they were not established in the things of God first.

3. **Zoë life: Life**
   a) the state of one who is possessed of vitality
   b) every living soul
   c) of the absolute fulness of life, both essential and ethical, which belongs to God, and through him both to the hypostatic "logos" and to Christ in whom the "logos" put on human nature
   d) life real and genuine, a life active and vigorous, devoted to God, blessed, in the portion even in this world of those who put their trust in Christ, but after the resurrection to be consummated by new accessions (among them a

more perfect body), and to last for ever.

John 10:10 verifies this anomaly.

There are many naysayers on this topic and I have heard them throughout my walk with Jesus on the prosperity messages of the church. I decree this is a deception that is widespread and it's so sad to live in poverty because your mind ain't right. We are to follow Jesus and keep His mind.

*1 Corinthians 2:16*
*For who hath known the mind of the Lord, that he may instruct him? but we have the mind of Christ.*

Stay focused on Jesus and stay in your own lane instead of looking over into mine as I walk blessed and favoured of God. I am His daughter and God the Father wants us to be blessed, not struggling in those worldly things. Get a grip people, poverty is not our portion but prosperity is. Why? Because we love God and He loves us. How do you treat those you love? How do you think God treats those He loves? Yes He does chasten but not your whole life. Some time we got to get a grip and want more. God wants to bless us and bless us in His abundance not mans'. Many find this hard to wrap their minds around but not me, I always embraced the blessed life God has offered me and my husband and family and we have never been disappointed. God has been so good to us He recently spoke to my heart to share this overflowing life with others so they may know and desire it too. So here I am trying to be obedient in God's beautiful things and prosperity is only one.

Let me verify all these substances with corresponding scriptures too.

## Abundance:

*1 Kings 18:41*
*And Elijah said unto Ahab, Get thee up, eat and drink; for there is a sound of abundance of rain.*

*Psalm 23:5*
*Thou preparest a table before me in the presence of mine enemies: thou anointest my head with oil; my cup runneth over.*

*Hosea 6:3*
*Then shall we know, if we follow on to know the LORD: his going forth is prepared as the morning; and he shall come unto us as the rain, as the latter and former rain unto the earth.*

*Haggai 2:9*
*The glory of this latter house shall be greater*
*than of the former, saith the LORD of*
*hosts: and in this place will I give peace,*
*saith the LORD of hosts.*

*Malachi 3:10*
*Bring ye all the tithes into the storehouse,*
*that there may be meat in mine house, and*
*prove me now herewith, saith the LORD of hosts,*
*if I will not open you the windows of heaven,*
*and pour you out a blessing, that there shall not*
*be room enough to receive it.*

*Matthew 25:29*
*For unto every one that hath shall be given, and*
*he shall have abundance: but from him that*
*hath not shall be taken away even that which*
*he hath.*

*Luke 6:38*
*Give, and it shall be given unto you; good*
*measure, pressed down, and shaken together,*
*and running over, shall men give into your*
*bosom. For with the same measure that ye mete*
*withal it shall be measured to you again.*

## Prosperity:

*Genesis 39:2*
*And the LORD was with Joseph, and he was
a prosperous man; and he was in the house of
his master the Egyptian.*

*Psalm 1:3*
*And he shall be like a tree planted by the rivers
of water, that bringeth forth his fruit in his
season; his leaf also shall not wither; and
whatsoever he doeth shall prosper.*

*Psalm 30:6*
*And in my prosperity I said, I shall never be
moved.*

*\*Psalm 35:27*
*Let them shout for joy, and be glad, that favour
my righteous cause: yea, let them say
continually, Let the LORD be magnified, which
hath pleasure in the prosperity of his servant.*

*Psalm 118:25*
*Save now, I beseech thee, O LORD: O LORD, I
beseech thee, send now prosperity.*

*Psalm 122:6*
*Pray for the peace of Jerusalem: they
shall prosper that love thee.*

*Jeremiah 29:11*
*For I know the thoughts that I think toward you, saith the LORD, thoughts of peace, and not of evil, to give you an expected end.*

*Zechariah 8:12*
*For the seed shall be prosperous; the vine shall give her fruit, and the ground shall give her increase, and the heavens shall give their dew; and I will cause the remnant of this people to possess all these things.*

*Philippians 4:19*
*But my God shall supply all your need according to his riches in glory by Christ Jesus.*

*\*3 John 1:2*
*Beloved, I wish above all things that thou mayest prosper and be in health, even as thy soul prospereth*

**Zoë Life:**

*Isaiah 55:1-3*

*1 Ho, every one that thirsteth, come ye to the waters, and he that hath no money; come ye, buy, and eat; yea, come, buy wine and milk without money and without price.*

*2 Wherefore do ye spend money for that which is not bread? and your labour for that which satisfieth not? hearken diligently unto me, and eat ye that which is good, and let your soul delight itself in fatness.*

*3 Incline your ear, and come unto me: hear, and your soul shall live; and I will make an everlasting covenant with you, even the sure mercies of David.*

*John 5:24*
*Verily, verily, I say unto you, He that heareth my word, and believeth on him that sent me, hath everlasting life, and shall not come into condemnation; but is passed from death unto life.*

*John 10:27-28*

*27 My sheep hear my voice, and I know them, and they follow me:*

*28 And I give unto them eternal life; and they shall never perish, neither shall any man pluck them out of my hand.*

*2 Peter 1:4*
*Whereby are given unto us exceeding great and precious promises: that by these ye might be partakers of the divine nature, having*

*escaped the corruption that is in the world through lust.*

*1 John 5:13*
*These things have I written unto you that believe on the name of the Son of God; that ye may know that ye have eternal life, and that ye may believe on the name of the Son of God.*

There are many scriptures to be found on: abundance, prosperity and the Zoë life in God. He has created this life for His children to be blessed and know the overflow of God. Have you ever overflowed by the Spirit of God? The reasoning for blessing us so we can overflow on others and give away what God has given us. The blessing is not primarily for us but to share with others so they too may be blessed and receive in their hearts what God has given them. It's available, so don't reject it today but receive ALL that God has to offer such as blessing and saving your children too. Will you reject this also?

*Psalm 37:25*
*I have been young, and now am old; yet have I not seen the righteous forsaken, nor his seed begging bread.*

*Isaiah 49:25*
*But thus saith the LORD, Even the captives of the mighty shall be taken away, and the prey of the terrible shall be delivered: for I will contend with him that contendeth with thee, and I will save thy children.*

These are beautiful things in God that He wants to share with you. Do you have faith enough to receive it all? Go for it God is our provider.

## Beautiful Things in a Dream…

On this Friday morning on July 23rd, 2021 I awoke with a beautiful snippet of a dream just before I opened my eyes. God knows exactly when to give me something so I will not forget it later. But it was short and sweet.

It looked like I received an email and this email was to be added to a story line I had for a book (this one perhaps?) and it was only a few lines with three strawberries as its header. I thought immediately this is very short and sweet and how am I going to make a story out of these few lines and fruit. So I got up from my dream and looked up strawberries in my dream interpretation book and it said: 1) Romance; 2) Love and friendship; 3) Good fruit; 4) Temptation: Scriptures:

1) *Song of Solomon 2:3 As the apple tree among the trees of the wood, so is my beloved among the sons. I sat down under his shadow*

*with great delight, and his fruit was sweet to my taste.*

2) As a heart-shaped fruit and sweet fragrance;

3) *Matthew 7:17 Even so every good tree bringeth forth good fruit; but a corrupt tree bringeth forth evil fruit.*

4) *Genesis 3:16 Unto the woman he said, I will greatly multiply thy sorrow and thy conception; in sorrow thou shalt bring forth. Children; and thy desire shall be to thy husband, and he shall rule over thee.*

That takes care of the strawberries which I thought were a sweet, romantic fruit between God and I; a good relationship. Now let's look at the number three: 1) God, the God-head 2) Complete 3) Resurrection 4) Perfection; 5) Divine fullness; 6) The Holy Spirit

We are going to make these three strawberries part of our logo because of this sweet dream, for Simply This Publishing. So every book going out will have this representation on the copyright page in the front of the book. Praise God! I had just asked my husband about a logo and my

dream came the next morning as sweet as can
be. Thank You Lord! This is an answer to prayer,
a beautiful dream.

## A Beautiful Things Prayer...

*Straight out of the Word we pray for you and yours:*

### *Ephesians 3:14-21*

*14 For this cause I bow my knees unto the Father of our Lord Jesus Christ,*

*15 Of whom the whole family in heaven and earth is named,*

*16 That he would grant you, according to the riches of his glory, to be strengthened with might by his Spirit in the inner man;*

*17 That Christ may dwell in your hearts by faith; that ye, being rooted and grounded in love,*

*18 May we be able to comprehend with all saints what is the breadth, and length, and depth, and height;*

*19 And to know the love of Christ, which passeth knowledge, that ye might be filled with all the fulness of God.*

*20 Now unto him that is able to do exceeding abundantly above all that we ask or think, according to the power that worketh in us,*

*21 Unto him be glory in the church by Christ Jesus throughout all ages, world without end. Amen.*

# AUTHOR"S CORNER

Susan J Perry lives and writes in Edgewater, Florida. She is married to John R Perry and they have 4 children in their blended marriage and 5 grandchildren who live all over the United States of America. They visit as much as they can.

She loves and serves her Lord Jesus Christ knowing only by His Spirit does she write and create page by page. Pure inspiration is so beautiful as the mornings run into nights and nights into mornings as she taps the keyboard on one finger quickly and as accurately as possible. She and her husband now publish books in *Simply This Publishing* and are having a great time doing so. Life is good for both of them. They give God all the praise, the honor and the glory for His loving ways. God is so good!

They have just started on children's books which are a new avenue for them and they hope it will work. They pray and ask God to direct their paths, and the funny thing is He does. God is in the blessing business and today is no different, God never changes, thankfully so.

They attend Edgewater Church of God in Edgewater, Florida with Bishop William T White and they love it there hearing the truth of God's Word. They are active in the church and are very thankful that they now serve locally, helping out as they are able.

Susan and her husband are ordained by Dr Frank and Karen Sumrall of Sumrall Global Ministries of Bristol, Virginia. Their life's call is in the Ministry of Helps to go into churches and help the Pastors wherever help is needed. They have an Aaron and Hur ministry of holding up the arms of the Pastors as they have need.

*Exodus 17:12*
*But Moses' hands became heavy; so they took a stone and put it under him, and he sat on it. And Aaron and Hur supported his hands, one on one side, and the other on the other side; and his hands were steady until the going down of the sun.*

Susan speaks at women's groups in churches when invited. She is now teaching one of her books in Sunday night classes in her own church: "Lessons In Deliverance." What a time they are having too! They often find themselves in Clearwater or Dunedin, Florida on the west coast while they live on the east coast and love every minute of it. They take their books and have a product table to set up wherever they go. She and her husband go where the Lord sends them and they are glad to do it. God always provides.

*Psalm 100:2*
*Serve the LORD with gladness; come before his presence with joy.*

# PERRY'S BOOK SHELF

## The Samaritan Woman Testifies
Kindle only: $9.95

## Simply This: The World's Greatest Message
Paperback: $5.95 Kindle: $3.99

## Preach It Sister Girl!
Paperback: $9.95 Kindle: $5.99

## ASK for WISDOM: The Safe Harbor of God
Paperback: $9.95 Kindle: $5.99

## A Stone's Throw Away: A Woman Testifies
Paperback: $12.95 Kindle: $6.99

**The Persistent Widow Testifies**
Paperback: $12.95 Kindle: $6.99

**The Woman Presenting the Alabaster Box Testifies**
Paperback: $12.95 Kindle: $6.99

**Great Holes in Your Pockets: Recovering All!**
Paperback: $9.95 Kindle $5.99

**Hidden in the Cleft of the Rock: A Woman Testifies**
Paperback: $12.95 Kindle: $6.99

**Daughters of Inheritance Testify**
Paperback: $12.95 Kindle: $6.99

**This Project is Called: HONOR**
Paperback: $9.95 Kindle: $5.99

**Our Experiences With ANGELS**
Paperback $9.95 Kindle $5.99

**The Double-Dip Blessings**
Paperback $9.95 Kindle $5.99

**It's Never Too Late To Pray**
Paperback $5.95 Kindle $2.99

### I AM A DUCK!
Paperback $9.95 Kindle $5.95

### The Woman Touching the Hem of His Garment Testifies
Paperback $12.95 Kindle $6.99

### This is the Anemic Church
Paperback $9.95 Kindle $5.99

### There is a Witness!
Paperback $9.95 Kindle $5.99

### Heal Them ALL! The Children's Portion
Paperback $7.95 Kindle $3.99

### Ye Shall Serve God Upon This Mountain!
Paperback $9.95 Kindle $5.99

### Thanksgiving Is Best!
Paperback $7.95 Kindle $3.99

### The ABC'S of Perry
Paperback for kids $12.95

### LOVE is Surely the Way
Paperback $7.95 Kindle $3.99

### Lessons In Deliverance
Paperback $12.95 Kindle $6.99

**Cancel Cancer: And The Effects Thereof**
Paperback $9.95 Kindle $5.99

**Royalty BELONGS To The Believer!**
Paperback $9.95 Kindle $5.99

**"Just When Did This Happen?"**
Paperback $9.95 Kindle $5.99

**I Declare Over You in Jesus Name**
Paperback $5.95 Kindle $3.99

**With Blessing & Favour**
**Will You Compass Me About!**
Paperback $9.95 Kindle $5.99

**Going Down The Barker Road Missing...**
Paperback $9.95 Kindle $5.99

**Deception of Man: Sin Lies At The Door**
Paperback $12.95 Kindle $6.99

**Beautiful Things: Out Of The Dust**
Paperback $9.95 Kindle $5.99

# CONTACT THE PERRYS

*1 Corinthians 14:3*
*But he who prophesies speaks edification and*
*exhortation and comfort to men*

All available on www.Amazon.com
Kindle Direct Publishing
*Simply This Publishing*
John & Susan Perry
Edgewater, Florida

## Contact info:

Susan J Perry, Email: susiebqt987p@yahoo.com
& Facebook; Simply This Publishing

John R Perry, Email: jperry8@bellsouth.net

## ALL BOOKS AVAILABLE ON AMAZON.COM

Books can also be ordered through bookstores
and big box stores if that is your preference.
There is always a way.

In Florida our books are available in:

**From My Library 2 URS**

**3510 S Nova Road, Suite # 107**

**Port Orange, Florida 32129**

# RESOURCES

Free black & white clipart

Wikipedia

Bible Gateway online

Various Bible translations as needed

Holy Spirit indwelling in inspiration and wisdom

Edgewater Church of God, perfect example

You tube Instrumental Music to write by

Various online Dictionaries

www.Amazon.com

No copyright infringement intended here

*The Joy of the Lord is my Strength!*

**_Psalm 48:2_**
**_Beautiful for situation, the joy of the whole earth, is mount Zion, on the sides of the north, the city of the great King._**

Made in the USA
Coppell, TX
24 September 2021

62907845R00087